Tell Me a Story

The Role of Narrative
in the Faith Life
of Catholics

ROBERT J. HATER

TWENTY
THIRD 23rd
PUBLICATIONS

Dedication

This book is dedicated to
my deceased parents, Stanley and Olivia Hater,
who taught me the meaning of our Catholic faith
and the depth of true love
through their love and dedication
to each other and to our family
and to all family members, past and present,
whose stories make possible the reflections in this book.

The Scripture passages contained herein are from the *New Revised Standard Version of the Bible*, ©1989, by the Division of Christian Education of the National Council of Churches of Christ in the U.S.A. Used by permission. All rights reserved.

Twenty-Third Publications
A Division of Bayard
One Montauk Avenue, Suite 200
New London, CT 06320
(860) 437-3012 or (800) 321-0411
www.23rdpublications.com

ISBN-10: 1-58595-552-3
ISBN 978-1-58595-552-7
Library of Congress Catalog Card Number: 2005910501

Contents

Foreword

Prolific writer Father Robert Hater often sees the underlying dynamics of a situation before these dynamics become apparent to others. Over the past three decades he has surfaced many pastoral issues years before these issues became topics of popular debate and reflection in parishes and schools. Father Hater surfaces pastoral issues again in this book, which seeks to reclaim an important but often misunderstood foundation of the Christian faith: the critical connection between what we believe, teach, and do as part of the Catholic faith tradition and what we experience in life.

As the author carefully demonstrates, a faithful Christian witness connects Church teaching, the stories of Scripture, and the Church's living Tradition (the source of belief) with reflection on personal experience, especially those experiences that serve as "defining moments" or "core life events." As a master storyteller and a pastorally-active theologian, Father Hater is uniquely suited to the task of exploring these connections.

This book is timely. The Catholic Church is struggling to articulate the relationship between human experience and the Church's doctrinal tradition. The nineteenth and twentieth centuries were marked by spiritual movements throughout the world and by a human hungering for spiritual experience. Spiritual exploration occurred both within and outside of formal religious traditions. The vibrancy of these movements put ancient religions, such as Roman Catholicism, somewhat on the defensive.

Contemporary, educated Christians need to know why the beliefs and principles of faith that guided previous generations should (or even can) become normative for people who face the challenges of the modern and postmodern world. Sociologist Wade Clark Roof studied the "spiritual questing" of the post-World War *doctrine vs. experience*

II baby boomer generation and found that a large proportion trust their spiritual experiences more than they trust the doctrinal traditions held by previous generations.

Vatican II recognized the spiritual movements of the nineteenth and twentieth centuries as basically good and reflective of the human yearning for God. But the council also emphasized the need for these movements to draw guidance from the wisdom of the past, from what the Catholic Church refers to as the "deposit of faith." The re-emphasis of the Church's doctrinal tradition, which has occurred in the several decades after the council and typified most dramatically in the release of a new *Catechism of the Catholic Church*, is part of an attempt to make the Church's wisdom more accessible.

Unfortunately many people do not know what to do with doctrine, while others are unsure what to do with human experience. This confusion has resulted in the inability of many religious leaders to articulate the relevance of their faith community's ancient wisdom. Father Hater offers a solution. He bridges the insights of both doctrine and human experience by exploring the role stories had in creating doctrine and the role doctrine can play in surfacing the religious meaning contained in stories, especially those stories of our most significant personal experiences.

Father Hater did not find this an easy book to write, even though as a seminary professor he knows the Church's doctrinal tradition inside and out; and as a parish priest, dynamic storyteller, and deeply compassionate and reflective man, he knows his way around human experience better than most. If the connections are not easy for him, then his struggle demonstrates how much work we must do in thinking about the interface between Church teaching and the spiritual experiences of people, and in particular how people express their experiences in the form of story.

In 2004 I invited Father Hater to conduct a lecture and workshop on the connection between story and doctrine at Loyola University New Orleans. Since he was so well received, and because his ideas sparked so much critical thinking on the part of his students, I encouraged him several times to write this book. I hope this book begins to stimulate new thinking on ways in which all Christians can breathe life into the creedal statements that shape the contours and parameters of our Christian faith.

We all have defining moments and core events. We express these moments and events in stories and these stories ultimately shape our identity. (I would even call this our "personal doctrines.") The author asks us to interpret the stories of our core moments in light of the story of Jesus Christ, and of the Church and its teachings. In so doing, our core life events, our defining moments, will become part of God's work to resurrect, from the ashes of loss, struggle, doubt, and death, a new creation that leads to meaningful living and the culmination of salvation history. Our stories become grafted into the grand story of God's loving initiative to transform our world.

For the author, the stories of Scripture and the lived Tradition of faithful believers through the centuries serve as a kind of radar screen for seeing God's activity in the world. Father Hater's book demonstrates a process for positioning the defining stories of his life on this radar screen so he can see God's presence in the events of his life. Throughout the book he uses core life experiences—a long, mysterious personal illness, the death of his father, the death of his mother, the stories of people he encountered in his ministry—to illustrate his process of rediscovering the role of story in shaping belief.

Father Hater models a way to connect Church teaching, the stories of Scripture and Tradition, and human experience. If we embrace his thoughts and try to emulate his example, our doctrines will become infused with the life and power they had for the early Christians. At the same time, the stories of our core events and defining moments will be revealed for what they truly are—powerful "in-breakings" of God's active love.

Father Hater's process leads to a Christianity that is both rooted in the wisdom of the past and intimately connected to the experience of God. It leads to evangelistic zeal, a zeal that has kept Christians on the front lines, making their families, communities, and world a better place.

Mark Markuly
Director of the Institute for Ministry,
Loyola University New Orleans

Introduction

Everyone loves a story. How many times have parents heard their children say, "Tell us a story!"? Teachers hold their classes in attention when they tell stories. Adults read novels and biographies. Civic festivals celebrate key moments in history. Telecommunications networks and the movie industry profit from our interest in stories. We track our genealogies and listen to the stories of our grandparents to learn who we are and who went before us. Every year Judaism and Christianity tell the great stories of their ancestors in faith.

I began to consider the importance of stories through a remark my mother made to me after she heard one of my homilies. I asked her how she liked it. She replied, "Bob, tell stories!" My mother's words burst my academic bubble. In effect, she told me that my abstract reflections on Scripture did not connect with her. I followed her advice and began telling stories in my homilies.

Soon I saw that the heart of the stories I told reflected Jesus' commandment of love. As I better identified the wisdom contained in my stories, their significance in terms of history became clearer. I connected personal, family, and communal stories with Jesus' stories. His stories affirmed my story, and at the same time conveyed God's eternal truths.

While reflecting on my story and my family's story, I realized that my mother told me many stories about Jesus. She also taught me to link my story with Jesus' story through my family and Church experiences. She told me the first stories that I heard as a boy and helped me to see that my family, parish, and the Church were essential components of my story. What an insight when I discovered that the stories my mother told me actually gave deeper meaning to my stories. I also saw in the Church's story the vital connections with basic Catholic teachings.

1

Every person has a story worth telling. I remember visiting an old woman in a retirement home who had no living relatives. She said, "The hardest part of living here is not the loneliness, but that there is no one interested in my story." Her words remind me of the beauty of each person's story.

This book considers "story" in two parts. Part One sets the foundation. The story of my mother's death is used to illustrate the connection between a story and basic belief. This section also discusses the key aspects of every story and the need to personalize basic belief. Chapter One presents three defining moments in my story and the three levels of meaning found in any story. Chapter Two discusses the story as lived, remembered, and told. It considers the changing elements of every story: time, place, person and community, and the unchangeable core of every story.

Chapter Three considers the defining moments or elements in Jesus' story: Jesus' humanity and divinity, the Trinity, and the Church as the Body of Christ. In addition, this chapter presents the theological and moral virtues that help believers live the Great Commandment; it also looks at responding to and celebrating Jesus' story. Chapter Four describes defining periods of Church history: the first controversies of the early Church, heresy and the Church Fathers, scholasticism and medieval theology, the Council of Trent, the Second Vatican Council, and the emerging global Church. This chapter identifies two essential principles in the relationship of story and belief.

Part Two looks more deeply into the nature of story and belief and how they connect with the three great theological virtues of faith, hope, and love. Chapter Five examines faith, the first of the theological virtues as well as story and personal presence, community, and belief. Chapter Six looks at story and basic belief through the lens of human meaning and the virtue of love. It points out why the story is important from the perspective of the Great Commandment and everyday living. Chapter Seven establishes a link between story, basic belief, and identity through hope. It does so from the vantage point of human identity and introduces three kinds of identity. It suggests hope as the motivator for relating story, basic belief, and life's meaning.

Each chapter concludes with items for reflection and action, presented in three sections: points for reflection, biblical passages for meditation or discussion, and action steps. Each section relates to the main themes and helps put into focus key ideas in the chapter. Adapt them to your needs.

Many people encouraged me to write this book. In addition, the following offered suggestions to improve the manuscript: Sr. Marge Kloos, SC, Traci Koenig, Debbie McGarry, Sandy Ogden, and Reverend Francis Voellmecke. I am especially indebted to Gwen Costello and Mary Carol Kendzia for their advice and suggestions while writing and finalizing the manuscript. Finally, I am deeply grateful to Mark Markuly for writing the Foreword to this book.

Connecting stories and basic belief is no easy task. Many of us fail to recognize that our stories contain disclosure points, places where God breaks into our history. Even if we recognize God in our stories, often we fail to connect basic Catholic beliefs with our stories. These connections take insight and vision, and they are particularly difficult to make today because many Catholics are ignorant of their basic beliefs.

This book is intended for anyone who wishes to appreciate how his or her story, Jesus' story, and the Church's story connect. These connections will help a person grow spiritually. Written from a Catholic perspective, the book's basic conclusions could be adapted to any religious tradition. This book is especially useful for parents, parish ministers, and theologians who convey the story of Jesus and the Church. Families and parish leaders help the Church community appreciate the relationship between story and belief in the light of God's kingdom. When these relationships are seen, faith sharing, catechesis, adult faith formation, and homilies take on new vibrancy.

Connecting Story and Belief

Story without basic belief is directionless,
while basic belief without story is lifeless.

Jim and Ellie looked lovingly at their infant child, admiring the mystery of this newborn. They were enraptured in the love that surrounded them. I asked them, "Do you think you produced Jason all by yourselves?" They became silent, surprised by the question, and then shook their heads "No" in unison.

When faced with life's mystery, we instinctively recognize the need to admit our limitations and search for the "more." This "more" includes the need to love and be loved, as well as the quest for God, our ultimate source. I experienced life's profound mystery through my mother's death, and I realized how her story connected with Jesus' story.

My Mother's Death

It was Monday of Holy Week. My mother could no longer eat or drink. She wanted to die a natural death and asked the doctor not to insert any tubes. Slowly, she weakened. By Holy Thursday, she no longer responded to us, her family, gathered by her bed. We thought she would die during the night as we kept vigil.

When Good Friday came, we wondered if she would die between twelve and three o'clock in the afternoon, the traditional time of Jesus' death. Her pulse eventually dropped to twelve beats a minute as her breathing became more labored. Our family remained in her room. I had decided to stay in the room until she died. My father died alone, and I wanted to be with my mother as she breathed her last breath.

At 4:30 in the afternoon, my sister said, "I think Mom wants to die alone. That's why she is hanging on. Let's leave the room." Reluctantly, I left. We returned, and my mother lived on. At 6:30 in the evening another family member remarked, "Let's go outside of the hospital and get some dinner. Maybe Mom wants us out of the building when she dies." The rest of the family left, but I stayed with her. Two religious sisters remained with me. My family was gone not two minutes when the strongest feeling came over me that I, too, should leave the hospital. One sister stayed at Mom's bedside, and the other left with me.

The sister and I went outside, bought a sandwich, and walked around the block. When we returned, the doctor was in the room. I immediately knew my mother had died. The religious sister, who had remained by her side, said that my mother breathed a silent, peaceful final breath, and that was it. She died no more than five minutes before I returned. I realized then that my mother had chosen to die apart from her family. She did not want to inconvenience us, even in death.

When I saw her dead body, I fell to my knees and sobbed, while praying for her. Kneeling there and holding Mom's lifeless hand, I imagined what Jesus' mother experienced when she held her son's body after he was taken down from the cross. In my mother's last days, she suffered her crucifixion. Now as I knelt next to her, overcome by grief, I did not think of resurrection.

On Easter Sunday my grief continued as the family celebrated an Easter Mass of Resurrection centered on my mother. During Mass I reflected on Jesus' story and his teaching about eternal life. This story and teaching were the ultimate ground for the hope that sustained me through her death. I believe she now enjoys eternal blessedness with God, her husband, Stanley, and her loved ones who preceded her in death.

My mother's death caused me to meditate on life's mystery from the vantage point of faith. I saw the relationship between my story, Jesus' story, and the Church's story, especially the teachings about death and resurrection. I saw Jesus' command to love God and one another lived out in her life. I better grasped the wisdom of her words, "Bob, tell stories" because her story disclosed the core message of God's kingdom of love. In her story I saw the virtues of faith, hope, and love in action.

During my grief following my mother's death, the Church's belief that God rewards those who lead good lives and die in Christ with eternal life consoled me. This teaching reinforces my confidence that because of my mother's good life on earth, she now enjoys eternal happiness in heaven. She is now free from pain and hurt. My faith enables me to see her suffering in light of Jesus' agony and death on the cross. His suffering validated her suffering, which she endured silently and without complaint. Faith discloses life's purpose and erases the notion that life is without meaning. My experience with my mother during her final days showed me the close link between story and basic belief. One without the other is incomplete.

My mother's death helped me to understand how stories provide a firm foundation for faith and belief. I also saw how hope gives us a reason to go on, and how love provides the energy to do so. God, who created us, is present in our lives and helps us connect the events in our stories with the events in Jesus' story. When our life stories are over, God calls us home to love for all eternity.

After my mother's comment about telling stories, I began to do just that. I looked for stories that reflected core messages. I connected Jesus' story and the Church's basic beliefs with such stories. I discovered that as my story unfolded, I recognized more clearly that I am a participant in a family, a neighborhood, a parish, a nation, and the world. My story is possible because of all the other stories that touch my life.

Key Aspects of Every Story

Stories can manifest life's deepest meaning. They are windows into both the mystery of life as well as the search for human meaning. Since life is complicated, there are many different windows to probe its meaning; likewise, there are many different types of stories.

What is it about a story that creates interest? There are four significant aspects to a story. First, stories are narrative descriptions. Many stories touch deep-seated aspects of human existence in imaginative ways. Stories use concrete images and describe specific times and places. Stories invite us to identify with their characters regardless of whether they are relatives or red birds. Once, after hearing one of my stories, an elderly man said, "The story you told wasn't your story alone, it was also my story." We may connect to the characters in a story with sympathy, compassion, resolve, fear, or disapproval. Stories engage our emotions and get our juices flowing.

Second, while every story links us in some way with the bigger human family, certain stories connect us with life's deepest dimensions. When we reflect we know that life involves more than money, sex, home, cars, and work. We know there is more to life, but we seldom put a name on it. The "more" that we desire touches a fundamental aspect of ourselves, and a core story is a powerful way to touch life's "something more."

Some people search for the "more" in sex, power, possessions, or drugs. Others seek to identify it through a rational, an analytic, or even a doctrinal approach. Life's core questions (Who am I? Where did I come from? Where am I going?) cannot be satisfied by such analytic efforts alone.

We often ask core questions when sitting with a dying parent or celebrating the birth of a child. In these moments, our cherished everyday world has less meaning. Birth and death offer us clues to our destiny; they are defining moments in our life. They can help us connect with the earth's story, the human story, Jesus' story, and the Church's story.

Third, core stories resonate deeply with us in an accessible way. When we hear them or read them, the mysteries of life, suffering, and death are more accessible. These mysteries are right in front of us. Core stories grab our head, heart, mind, and feelings in a holistic way. In so doing, stories engage the whole person.

When my mother suggested that I tell stories, I began to see life in a new way and appreciate better the Great Commandment to love God and love our neighbor. Before that time, I taught people the content of the Catholic faith or basic belief. I gave little attention to life's other dimensions, including its emotional element. I focused on only one side of the coin, namely, the basic beliefs. Once I began to tell stories, I looked at both sides of the coin, the holistic value of stories. A good story addresses the whole person, not only the head. A good story unites, as it were, both the head and the heart in a real encounter with life.

Fourth, stories flow out of community experiences and return us to community. Family stories connect us to the past and invite us to continue the family's traditions. One family member's story often resonates with other family members' stories. This resonance is especially true of major life events, like the death of a parent. Civic stories recount our country's heroes and help us better appreciate our role in the community, and stories from Church history help us appreciate our role as Church members.

Both story and basic belief are necessary to live a well-balanced life. Human experience, which stories reflect, is the center point.

mes experiences are interpreted by touching stories. At times, abstract, precise doctrinal statements, like "Jesus is fully God and fully man," express the core of an experience. The Church's basic beliefs are derived from the story of Jesus through analysis and reflection.

Making Basic Beliefs Personal

From a faith perspective, the human story begins with God's love, is reflected in creation, reaches fulfillment in Jesus' story, continues in the Church's story, and is experienced in family stories. God's love is personalized in our stories and the saints' stories, and formulated in the Church's basic teachings. I learned how basic Catholic beliefs related to my story as I grew up in my family, neighborhood, and parish. Jesus' story and basic Catholic beliefs influenced my story.

My stories enabled me to better appreciate the truths contained in Jesus' stories. From childhood I believed in Jesus and the Church. Experiences such as my mother's death personalized my beliefs in a new way. I now see that *story without basic belief is directionless, while basic belief without story is lifeless.* Either without love is pointless. We need both.

When either story or basic belief is neglected, personal and Church life lacks balance. Both story and basic belief are important in different ways. Our stories make our basic beliefs personal. Basic beliefs connect with our core experiences and clarify the core elements of our stories.

The New Testament began with the experience of early followers of Jesus. The gospel stories and lessons are communal reflections based on Jesus' life, God's dealings with his chosen people in the Old Testament, and the experience of the early Church. The New Testament contains key elements of Christian community's story, from which emerge the Church's basic beliefs. The New Testament story sets a solid direction for our stories. At the same time, our stories and the faith stories of others help keep the biblical stories fresh and alive.

The interface of story and basic belief sometimes begins with a story. This approach is called "theology from within." The interface can begin also with basic belief, which is referred to as "theology from without." The remaining chapters in Part One address both perspectives.

Part One is divided into four chapters. Chapter One looks at defining moments in my story. Chapter Two discusses the story as lived, remembered, and told, while Chapter Three explores defining aspects of Jesus' story. Chapter Four reflects on defining dimensions of Church history. The unifying thread of these chapters is the Great Commandment.

Defining Moments in My Story

Now to him who by the power at work within us is able
to accomplish abundantly far more than all we can ask
or imagine, to him be glory in the church and in Christ Jesus
to all generations, forever and ever. Amen. (Eph 3:20–21)

Paul's prayer speaks of God's influence in the entirety of our lives. We find God's divine presence at key moments in our lives. In Part One, the story about the new parents and the story of my mother's death describe defining life moments. This chapter examines three defining moments in my story and explores the various levels of a story's meaning. The following stories occur in God's time (*kairos*), rather than in human time (*chronos*). God's time requires patient waiting. Waiting provides the space for God's grace to take root so that basic belief can be sensed as well as learned.

Three Defining Moments

When I think of my life story, three defining moments come to mind. They touch my core because in them God touched me through love. The first moment is my prolonged illness over thirty years ago, the second is my father's death in 1980, and the third is my mother's death in 2001. Each moment refocused my priorities and set me on a new course. Each helped me better appreciate God's command to love. Friends who know me recognize these experiences as key moments in my life. After each one, my friends saw me change.

My Prolonged Illness

A prolonged sickness in the late 1960s reshaped my life. Prior to my illness, I worked hard and tried to lead a good life. Looking back today, I see that my life was quite superficial.

At age thirty-three I became sick following an automobile accident. After a brief hospital stay, I returned home. Although the doctor said I was okay, I became sicker and sicker. My strength ebbed as I sat month after month in my room. Weakness turned into depression, which left me on the verge of despair. I was thrown into a swirl of doubt. Everything I once cherished—athletic prowess, intelligence, determination, confidence, popularity—left me. I could hardly walk, my attention span shortened, and my energy to play sports dissipated. I did not want to see anyone, and I spent my time sitting alone in my room.

The inner pain was more excruciating than the bodily weakness. No one, including the doctors, knew what was wrong. During these weeks and months, I often stared at a wall. My only consolation was the crucifix that hung in my bedroom. As I meditated upon it, I thought, "If you can make it, so can I." I would often repeat this mantra while pounding my head on the wall, hoping to alleviate the pain. I saw divine love hanging on a piece of wood. I better appreciated my faith and the need for hope. I became almost immobilized and saw no way out except for abandonment to God.

After four years of such hell I gradually regained my strength, and then I suffered a relapse. This time the doctors operated and discovered the physical cause of my sickness. After surgery it took nine years before I could speak of what happened during my illness. No one knows what it means to come to the limits of personal endurance and not give up except through personal experience. Only faith, hope, and love of my family and a few friends saved me.

During this defining moment, I sifted out what was important. I suffered a long "agony in the garden and crucifixion." My priorities changed. Sickness and its aftermath led me on an inner journey that still continues. The most striking lessons I learned were about myself. Since I experienced brokenness, it is easier now for me to support the poor, marginalized, and neglected members of society and the Church. I better appreciate what is necessary to be saved—love God and one another.

My Father's Sickness and Death

The second defining moment in my life was my father's prolonged sickness and death. When he became ill in 1979, I was on a year sabbatical at Notre Dame University. I had scarcely arrived there when he was taken to the hospital. I needed to decide whether to continue my sabbatical or return to my dying father. I choose the latter. After my sickness a few years earlier, the decision to stay with my father was no decision at all; it was a foregone conclusion. I longed to be with him and to love him.

In the ensuing months, I dealt with the grief of seeing him immobilized in a hospital bed. I dealt with the insensitivity of people, including parish ministers, who told me to get on with my life and return to Notre Dame. One individual said, "You only have one year to do your professional thing. You're giving this up. You'll never have another chance like this. Why don't you go back?" I was too hurt to reply, but thought to myself, "You don't get it. My Dad is dying. I have to be with him. It's the least I can do for him after a lifetime of love and sacrifice for me and our entire family."

I count this choice to stay home as a pure gift of grace. It was a defining life moment for me. Month after month, sitting at my father's bedside enabled me to acknowledge what is of real value. Spending time with him and with my mother helped me establish deep life priorities. These priorities come down to love. This time with my father also made me recognize the human limitations of religious institutions when it comes to connecting Jesus' story with the stories of broken men and women like my father. How tragic when love seems absent from our churches and when Christians hurt one another. How contrary to the Great Commandment.

My Mother's Death

My third defining moment is time that I spent with my mother before she died. This event, more than any other, refocused my interior life and put me in contact with the deep bonds of love between a son and his mother that cannot be described, only classified as God's blessing.

People who do not know me might say, "You did not include your ordination to the priesthood in your defining moments. Why not?" To be sure, ordination was a pivotal moment for me, but of a different order than the three described above. My ordination began a journey that I have followed for over forty years. It sets the parameters for my prayer life and service to God's people. But the three defining moments in my life taught me how to respond as a priest, with love and forgiveness.

Theologically, ordination effected a basic shift in my relationship with the Trinity and the Church. This spiritual shift was built on my human nature. In the order of nature, the foundation for the order of grace, my sickness and the death of my father and mother are defining life moments. They disclosed the depths of love, faith, and hope—central virtues for every Christian, especially leaders of Christ's Church.

By itself, ordination did not change me as a man. It did not make me any more or less human. It did not teach me why to love, how to have faith, or how to hope. The defining moments mentioned above affected the core of who I am as a "man-child" of God. I would still be a man if I were not an ordained priest, but I would not be effective as a priest if I lost sight of my humanness. Through these three defining moments the Holy Spirit, who called me in baptism and specified this call at my ordination, now assists me in giving leadership as a priest in the Church by praising God and serving God's people through love. These defining moments taught me to see myself first as Bob Hater, needing love, faith, and hope, and subject to the joys, hopes, aspirations, temptations, sickness, and limits of every human being. Only in this light, as a sinner needing God's redemption, can I appreciate my calling as an ordained priest.

These defining moments enabled me to identify key aspects of meaning that the story embraces. These aspects are the secondary, community, and core levels or dimensions of meaning. Each is necessary, and no story exists without them. While interrelated, they differ.

Secondary Level of Meaning

Before getting sick, my priorities centered on secondary things. I was into sports, looked for recognition and honors, and needed to be "number one." I prayed and celebrated the Eucharist, but other things easily distracted me. My sickness changed my priorities. The same thing happened when my father was dying. The meaning that I could derive from the learning and contacts that I made on my sabbatical mattered little in light of my father's illness.

Secondary meaning is necessary. It is the meaning found in everyday things, occupations, and desires. Our cars, homes, money, clothing, and workplaces have meaning. We cannot live without the functional part of life. When the doctors finally diagnosed my problem, it was a blessing for me. They used medical procedures to do so. When Dad was dying, medication prolonged his life. Many "things" are vital parts of our lives.

When material things, power, or prestige become ends in themselves, however, they fail to fulfill their purpose and lead to alienation. Material things, power, or prestige by themselves never move us to a deeper level of life.

Communal Level of Meaning

We derive meaning from human interaction, especially community relationships. The word "community" includes a variety of relational patterns—family, friends, and Church.

During my sickness, the people that came to offer me comfort and those who never came surprised me. Many friends, whom I hoped would come, never came or called. Other people, whom I did not expect, provided great support. From such visits, I learned much about how people deal differently with sickness. I realized that some people have difficulty in being with sick people. Above all, I realized that being present with sick people, without words, can touch the core dimension of who they are. Often presence is the best way to love. After all, isn't that what Mary and John did at the foot of the cross?

Ordinary people comforted me the most when I was sick. In them I discovered the real meaning of the Great Commandment. I also found special comfort in my family's love. They never questioned or avoided me.

The support and love that our family gave my mother during her last days continued the love we shared throughout life. The love reflected by our family at my mother's death began with my parent's dedication to us. They sacrificed position, money, and personal comfort to raise us in a loving Catholic home. Our summer vacations solidified family relationships. Dad hid twenty dollars each week under a drawer in the bedroom to allow us to travel on vacation. The money that some parents spent on themselves to eat out, our parents saved for our holidays. During childhood we were together most of the time. Even the arguing and disagreements between my brother, sisters, and me taught us life's give and take. Our home was a community of faith and love, which prepared us for a life of service.

We need community. In a society where family roots are weak and members spread around the globe, loving communities can touch the core of who we are. When family ties are weak, we especially need the Church to manifest God's kingdom of love. Since every human is part of various communities (family, work, parish, neighborhood), community stories that support, reinforce, and help us identify core elements in our story are especially useful.

Core Level of Meaning

A story's communal and secondary dimensions point to a story's core dimensions. At this level, one person's story becomes every person's story. While the secondary level differs significantly from person to person, and the community level varies from community to community, the core level manifests what is the same in all humans because it is rooted in God and centered in the need for love.

Our questions, hopes, fears, and aspirations are held in common. We discover this level of meaning in the quietude of our souls and the depths of who we are. A story expresses this dimension of life in a way that rational discourse cannot. Stories make us laugh or cry, smile or frown. They make us sit up and take notice because they disclose an intimate and eternal aspect of each person.

All humans search for ultimate meaning and ask core questions. Who am I? Why was I born? Why do I have to suffer? What happens when I die? Is there meaning in my life? The core dimension enables us to connect with other people, identify our gifts, and search for God.

When I sat with my mother during her last hours, I identified with the core level in a way that I never had before. The woman who bore me in her womb for nine months and loved me through her life was dying. Her suffering wrenched me. Why should I expect less pain at her death than she suffered when I was born? During my birth and at her death, resurrection and new life followed our suffering. The core level of meaning gives a story its life.

The three defining moments of my sickness, my father's death, and my mother's death connected my story and my Catholic belief in a powerful way. They enabled me to see more deeply God's footprints in my life. They also keep me looking more deeply into the story as lived, remembered, and told, which is the theme of Chapter Two.

Points for Reflection

- What experiences have allowed you to see life's priorities in a different light? Why?

- Identify a defining moment in your personal life. How did this moment make a difference in your life? What significant life changes resulted?

- What defining moments are in your family life? How did these moments affect the relationships in your family?

- Consider your professional life. Have you had a defining moment in your professional life? What change resulted from this moment?

- Connect a defining moment in your life with an event in Jesus' life.

- What have you found most helpful as you adapt to life's inevitable difficulties, failures, and suffering? Think of the role that faith, family, friends, and parish each play in your life.

- How can reflecting on your defining moments strengthen your relationship with your family, your friends, and God?

- Are family members and others alienated from you or your family because of what happened in the defining moments in your life or their lives? Why? How can reconciliation begin?

- Which of your stories has the most meaning? What does this story say about the direction of your life?

Biblical Passages for Reflection

- Read the passion account of Jesus in the Gospel of John (18—19). Ask God for the grace to endure difficult times as Jesus did.

- Imagine Mary's feelings after Jesus died. Connect what she endured to painful moments in your life.

Action Steps

Lessons learned. With a friend discuss something you learned from the author's story of his mother's death or of his prolonged illness. Are there similar stories in your life?

Family discussion. Gather members of your family together. Explain the meaning of a defining moment and ask each family member to identify one or two defining moments. Ask what each person and what the whole family can learn from such moments. Are there any connections to stories of our faith, to basic Christian beliefs, or to the events in Jesus' life?

Visit elderly persons. Arrange to visit elderly persons in retirement homes or in their own homes. Invite them to share important stories from their past with you. If appropriate, ask them if you could read a story of Jesus to them that has similarities to the story told to you.

Chapter Two

Story Lived, Remembered, and Told

They are to do good, to be rich in good works,
generous, and ready to share. (1 Tim 6:18)

Every story is lived, remembered, and told. A story implies a process and a history. Among earthly creatures, we alone can tell stories and appreciate them because we are symbol-making animals, capable of self-reflection, love, compassion, and forgiveness. Since we can move beyond ourselves in thought and words, we can appreciate our history and our connection with creation. Stories help us sort out our uniqueness.

We better understand our stories by putting them in a communal and historical context: the time that the story takes place, the place where it happens, the persons involved, and the community that influences the story's outcome. Context influences every story, as seen in Maria's story below. (A missionary nun, who was in Maria's country after the war and had met Maria, told me this story.)

Story as Lived: Maria's Story

Maria grew up behind the Iron Curtain in a Communist country that once was predominantly Catholic. When the Communists took over, they killed many religious men and women and shipped others to concentration camps. In Maria's town the Communists permitted a few priests to celebrate Mass. Other public displays of the faith, however, were forbidden. Catechetical instruction was kept to a minimum and often took disguised forms. Young Catholics knew little about their faith beyond what their parents taught them.

When Maria was a young woman, the most popular single man in town courted her. She seriously considered marrying him, but felt God was calling her in another direction. She did not know what this meant. Maria discussed her call with her pastor, who put her in contact with a group of young women who were studying the literature of Benedictine women mystics in a poetry class.

After meeting with this class for some time, Maria asked her pastor where she could learn more about the lifestyle described in the books the class read. The priest introduced her to a woman, an engineer in town, and they became friends. One day the woman invited Maria on a journey with her to a distant part of the country. On their way the woman told Maria that she was a religious sister. When they arrived at their destination, Maria met the superior of this order. Only then did Maria learn that the young women's "poetry class" served as her novitiate. Some in this class, impressed by the Benedictine lifestyle, were invited to join the community. Their instruction occurred in the utmost secrecy. When Maria signed her final vow papers, the superior immediately burned them, so as to leave no records that the event took place.

Maria returned home and got a job in business. At work she shared God's love. Until the fall of the Soviet bloc countries, the only religious women she knew were the sister in her hometown and the superior, neither of whom she saw again after her vow ceremony. Maria's mother and father never knew their daughter was a consecrated religious woman.

After the Communists fell, she finally met other sisters in her community. Some even lived near her. Maria began living a communal life. Her religious community had to start from the beginning. Once they came together, many of the sisters discovered that they had developed a similar spirituality centered on a strong devotion to the Holy Spirit and rooted in the Great Commandment. This spirituality was honed during long years of persecution. These women depended on the Spirit's wisdom to keep them going.

Maria's story reveals God's loving presence in her life. Her story, like every story, has four aspects: time, place, person, and community.

Time. Maria's experience occurred in a distinct period of time. The Communist takeover of a once-Catholic country set the stage for Maria's story. The Communists refocused the lives of their citizens and radically affected the people's attitudes, actions, and beliefs.

Place. The situation in Maria's country under Communism affected her religious formation. The way this formation came about was largely unknown to her. It was under the inspiration of the Holy Spirit and rooted in the love of her own family. (In other parts of the world, strict rules, approved by Rome, regulated the formation programs of women religious. But Maria never left the secular world. Many women religious in other places left the world so completely that, when their social context changed after Vatican II, they found it difficult to adjust to new directions in religious life.)

Person. Maria listened to her call by the Holy Spirit, a power greater than herself. The Spirit guided Maria in ways often hidden to her. She did not even know that she was being subtly prepared for her calling through reading and studying the Benedictine mystics. If she had not responded by becoming a nun, this Benedictine spirituality would have served her as a mother or single professional woman.

As Maria studied the mystics, God's footprints on her soul became more apparent. These footprints were signs of God's presence in her through her conception, birth, baptism, Eucharist, and through the faith, hope, and love of her family.

Community. In Maria's case, a small community of the priest and two nuns affirmed and directed her call. Maria now spends her days learning more intimately about the God who called, inspired, and protected her during her silent years. Living with the women in her religious community and discussing her experiences with them, she now sees these silent years in light of the God who called her.

The Unchangeable Core of Every Story

Her story, like my mother's story related in Part One, invites us to look at how God is present in our lives. Reflection helps us appreciate both God's love and human love in new ways. When I held my mother's hand in the hospital room after she died, I better understood why all life is summed up in love. I remembered when I failed to express my love for her. I also appreciated why Jesus taught us the way of love. By admitting the human limits that are manifested in our stories, we gain new insights into our never-ending quest for God and truth.

As we change we sense that something more is around life's corner. The four aspects (time, place, person, and community) of story indicate why our earthly story always changes. When one aspect changes the story changes and our identity shifts focus. Life's ever-shifting sands cry out for a permanent, unchanging core. We discover this core in Jesus, who offers us a firm rock upon which to build our life on earth and our future in eternity.

Both my mother's story and Maria's story illustrate that each life is based on a fundamental orientation that sets the direction a person's life takes. For example, my mother grew up in a free society and Maria in an oppressive Communist world. Both came from Catholic homes, and this fundamental orientation influenced their lives. In my mother's case, family and public prayer were integral to who she was. In Maria's case, family prayer occurred in secrecy because public worship, beyond Sunday Mass, was forbidden. The community dimension (living in a country that did or did not allow public prayer) is different, but the need to love and be loved remained the same for both Mom and Maria.

On the core level no outside force controls our ability to opt for God and to discover meaning in any given circumstance, even in an oppressive one. Heroic people who suffer under persecution, like Maria, and those who endure pain silently, like my mother, reveal our common humanity.

Our stories never happen in isolation. We are members of many communities, beginning with our family. Our stories come out of these communities and, in turn, impact them. The story of my mother's death had profound consequences for all our family, as well as for my mother's other relatives and friends. Both my father's death and my prolonged sickness also had great impact on others, as did the story of Maria's faith described above. In fact, every story has an impact on other people.

The person who dies alone in a retirement home or on the street still belongs to the human community. When someone lonely dies, all of us need to grieve.

I saw the depths of human bonding while serving as the chaplain of a nursing home for destitute people. I remember one old woman who waited for me every Friday, just to touch my hand. I recognized her dignity as a human being, but I never learned the facts of her story. Her grasping attempt to reach out to me revealed that our stories are connected on a much deeper level than that of family. Everyone is united in God.

This woman's feeble efforts to connect with life never left me, even though I forgot her name many years ago. I will always remember her halting, frail hand struggling to reach out and touch my arm, despite being too weak to speak. Her efforts, as she neared the end of her life story, profoundly changed my attitude toward the sick and frail. One Friday morning I did not see her in the corridor, and I knew she had died. Although I never saw her again her spirit remains with me and inspires me to reach out to those in need.

Story as Remembered

We cannot fully recapture a story; our experiences cannot be put completely into words. Even so, each story still hints at a person's or group's fundamental direction on issues like death, meaning, identity, and suffering.

People often understand the same story in different ways. Memories of a story differ from person to person and from community to community. Each member of my family remembers my mother's last days differently, but all our stories are rooted in her love of God and of our family. The differences come from our unique relationship with her. Although her death affected each of us differently on a secondary (non-essential) and community (interpersonal) level, we reacted the same way on the core level. We grieved her loss, and beyond our different expressions of grief, we felt love, loss, and loneliness. Such core experiences bonded us into mutual affection and support.

Our unity on the core level was most evident during the preparations for her funeral and the Mass of Christian Burial. We celebrated her wonderful life, confident that she was now with God. The secondary dimensions of selecting the music, arranging the program, and dressing her were our tribute, showing our love for her. We wanted my mother's faith-filled, joyful burial to be an expression of her love.

Something similar is true when a story's details fade or when the story is told by different people. For example, although each evangelist recounted Jesus' story differently, each told the story of our redemption through Jesus' core experiences of suffering, death, and resurrection. Each rendition of Jesus' story reflects the Great Commandment as the center of his teaching. The evangelists did not intend to literally recount his life, but constructed the gospels to fit their purposes. They indicated in different ways what is necessary to follow Jesus' path to eternal life. Interpreters sift out the intentions and circumstances of each gospel to get to the story's core dimensions.

No story happens in a vacuum. Neither is it remembered in a vacuum. All stories have imbedded values; no story is value-free. The story conveys values that the storyteller intends to convey. Each storyteller emphasizes certain things and minimizes others. This emphasis and minimization is done while keeping in mind the audience and the circumstances

Story as Told

Remembering a story and telling it are closely associated. When Maria told her story about life under Communist rule, she emphasized the story elements most significant to her. The same thing happens when I tell my mother's story. When I talk about my mother with caregivers in retirement homes or hospitals, I stress the aspects of the story that center on how professional nursing or pastoral people treated her and our family. Giving specific instances, I describe how a nurse or minister loved and supported us. I also mention the example of a caregiver from an organization that had a great reputation who treated us coldly. When I address this core level, I avoid implicating individuals or groups.

Stories reflect the customs, language, and rituals of the times in which they happened. Those hearing a story are aided greatly if they are acquainted with the story's context. Scripture study, which addresses the context of the text, helps the reader better appreciate God's revealed Word.

Many stories are embellished. Exact details are often not absolutely essential. Details relate to the secondary level of meaning. The values a story conveys pertain to core meaning. Many different stories can have the same core message. For example, the four gospels each tell the core story of Jesus in a different way. Each variation depends not only on the evangelist, but also on the community for which the gospel was intended. What is stressed in a story geared to one community (Jewish converts) might not be so important in a story directed primarily to a Gentile audience.

God's Footprints

Both my mother's story and Maria's are significant for those who believe in Jesus. Their families, deeply grounded in the Catholic tradition, set the foundation for their life journeys. Their stories help us realize that we do not come to God in a vacuum.

We have to believe that God exists and know something about God before we can decide to accept Jesus' revelation. We may sense a basic desire for God deep within us. Maria's search for more in life manifested a yearning for God. Creation stories, cave paintings, and rituals of early peoples reflect this same yearning. People call the object of their yearning by different names.

Paul writes about the search for God by non-believers. He says that God has been revealed plainly to them (Rom 1:19–20). He goes on to explain that from the beginning of creation, God's deity and power, though invisible, have been present for humans to see in God's creation. Creation discloses God's footprints and prepares for God's incarnation in Christ. The Old Testament clearly revealed God's footprints; Yahweh's love entered history and spoke through holy men and women. God's love of the Jewish people in the Old Testament is refocused by Jesus in the New Testament as God's inclusive love of all people.

We can find God's footprints in all people's stories. The closer we get to the core of human existence—birth, love, celebration, suffering, death, resurrection—the clearer God's footprints become. Since each of us are made in God's image, God dwells at the heart of each story. Our lived story manifests God's presence and sets the stage for God's revelation in Scripture and in our relationships with creation, community, and Church. In learning the ways that God communicates with us, family takes center stage, because it powerfully influences our image of God.

God Is Present in Every Person's Story

A rich man named Edwin once berated me because I did not accept a large cash donation from him after a prolonged counseling session. As he pushed a hundred-dollar bill at me he said, "Take the money, everyone gets paid for their time." When I answered that I freely give my time because of my faith, he blurted out, "You really helped me. Take it, take it! Don't you know that money is the only thing that really counts?"

This man, rich in earthly goods, was poor. He never appreciated love. Edwin's thinking was distorted. He neglected his family, never went to church, and displaced his desire for the true God with the god of money. The extremes to which he went in his pursuit of wealth left him hollow and unfulfilled.

Even though people like Edwin can freely turn away from God, their choice never destroys their innate desire for God. Money, success, power, material things, drugs, and alcohol cannot fulfill this desire. Tragic, indeed, when created things, instead of the Creator, become a person's ultimate goal. Many people deify a functional lifestyle. They glory in this world and pay little attention to their spiritual well-being. They displace God and become alienated from their life's purpose. Sometimes, with God's grace, a spiritual retreat or good pastoral care can bring God back into a person's life.

Even though materialism and secularism often permeate a person's story, God still loves that person. In every materialistic-minded individual, beautiful, godlike qualities exist. Often these qualities take form in generosity to the poor, in striving for justice, or in honesty in business.

To find God's loving footprints we can look anywhere: in the marketplace, in neighborhoods, prisons, drug rehabilitation centers, hospitals. God is present in every person's story, even when the person denies God's presence. No matter who we are or what we do, the desire for God remains, even though this desire may be sidetracked. This desire constantly invites us to search for the true God of heaven and earth.

When reflecting on a child's birth, a spouse's sickness, or a parent's death, we return to life's mystery. This mystery at the core of our stories challenges us to examine what is important. Considering a story through the lens of faith can help us see through the eyes of Christ rather than through the eyes of the world.

Life's Meaning Revealed by Jesus

We cannot appreciate Jesus as the full revelation of God without first acknowledging God's existence revealed in creation. God's footprints became clear to me during the three defining moments of my life. By connecting Jesus' story to our innate desire for God we can recognize God's loving plan for our redemption accomplished through Jesus' life, death, and resurrection.

Creation, various philosophical systems, and different religious traditions reflect God's light. The Old Testament reveals the light as the one true God. In the New Testament God is fully revealed in Jesus. "What has come into being in him was life, and the life was the light of all people. The light shines in the darkness..." (Jn 1:3b–5). This light is present in our lives. Whenever we search for absolute values of conduct, this light moves us. Even before we confess that "Jesus is Lord, the Son of God," this light is present in a clouded way.

Since our stories reflect God's light, our stories invite us to recognize that Jesus' story contains the ultimate manifestation of life's meaning. This ultimate meaning centers on love, which we recognize in the traces of God in our stories. In so doing, we can better appreciate Jesus. His teachings on love, forgiveness, justice, and compassion touch the core of our stories and reveal the final goal of our striving—to be with God.

Other than the glimpses of God's nature that we get from creation, revelation, and our stories, the mystery of God remains couched in uncertainty. Only when we see God face to face in the beatific vision will we fully know why Jesus calls us to love God and our neighbor. In the meantime, Jesus reveals aspects of God that we cannot discover by reason. This is the topic of Chapter Three.

Points for Reflection

- Reflect on your priorities. Do you feel that your fundamental orientation sets up any barriers to how others relate to you? Give examples.

- Which of your defining moment stories has the most meaning to you? What does this story say about your life's fundamental orientation?

- How would you describe you inner quest for God? How often do you think of ultimate aspects of life like suffering and death? How healthy is your attitude toward such issues? Are you afraid to face such issues?

- What consolation does Jesus' story give you when dealing with the sickness or death of a loved one or dealing with your failures and pain?

- How does reflection on life's mystery move you to express praise and thanks to God?

- In reading the stories in this chapter, which of your stories do they bring to mind?

- Does your story or your family's story include a pregnancy out of marriage, addiction, or drugs? How can Jesus' story and your basic Christian beliefs give insight and comfort to such experiences?

- Remember your favorite story. Reflect on its meaning. Why does it have special significance? What does this significance tell you about your life?

- What values and strengths exist in your family as a result of connecting your family's story and Jesus' story?

- What is the most important insight that you gleaned from this chapter? Why does it have special significance? What does it tell you about your life?

Biblical Passages for Reflection

- In reflecting on your stories, what stories from Jesus' life come to mind?

- Which gospel stories have helped you hear God's voice and relate the gospel to your experiences?

- Read Genesis 1:1–27. What consequences does the truth that you are made in God's image have for you personally and for the way you treat others?

Action Steps

Heal family hurts. Family members may suffer from division and separation at some point. Reflect on a person in your family who is not involved with the family. Pray for this person, asking God to help you understand the reasons why this person is not involved. Ask for guidance in healing the relationship.

Celebrate family stories. Discover interesting aspects of your family's story by asking parents, grandparents, or older adults to tell stories. Retell to other family members the stories you think they might enjoy.

Visit elderly persons. Arrange to visit elderly persons in retirement homes or in their own homes. Invite them to share important stories from their past with you. If appropriate, ask them if you could read a story of Jesus to them that has similarities to the story told to you.

Remember and act. Remember the support you received during a difficult time. Plan to help someone in a similar circumstance. Look first to the needs of your family and friends.

Chapter Three

Defining Elements of Jesus' Story

As you therefore have received Christ Jesus the Lord,
continue to live your lives in him, rooted and built up in him and
established in the faith, just as you were taught,
abounding in thanksgiving. (Col 2:6–7)

The following story reflects the gratitude of appreciative towns-people who came to know the living Christ and live according to the dictates Paul gave to the Colossians. (The story is based on a story told by someone with knowledge of the town; the origin of the story is unknown.)

Once there was a small Siberian town in which was located a brutal Russian gulag, or prison. Sorrow and despair permeated this place, a place where the streets were paved with the ashes and bones of dead prisoners. The people had little hope. After the Russian revolution of the 1990s brought freedom, Christianity returned. Still, the people found it hard to believe that freedom was possible.

One day a Russian orthodox priest arrived in the town and began rebuilding the church. A remarkable thing happened at the first eucharistic celebration. When the priest proclaimed the Word of God from the sacred books, people cried and sobbed throughout the church. Many in attendance had never heard the gospel message of hope. After the liturgy, they said the service was the most beautiful thing they had ever witnessed in their town. Jesus' words, announcing liberation from suffering, sin, and death, gave them new life. Their tears were tears of hope and joy, not those of death and despair. The citizens of this small Siberian town truly heard "good news."

As this community continued to study God's Word, they learned of God's love and of the Son who was sent to die for their sins to give them eternal life. They learned that God is always with them, providing the strength and courage to face life's struggles. For the first time, they heard of God's covenant promise of fidelity and Jesus' teaching on the Great Commandment of love.

This chapter concerns Jesus' story. What are the defining elements of his story? What is our response to Jesus' story? How do we celebrate Jesus' story? As with the Siberian townspeople, Jesus' story also deeply affects my story. Without faith in him as the Son of God, my life makes little sense.

I. Defining Aspects of Jesus' Story

There are elements in his story that are theologically defining moments for me. These defining theological elements are Jesus' divinity and humanity, the Trinity, and the Church as the Body of Christ.

Jesus' Divinity and Humanity

Jesus' divine and human natures, the first defining aspect of his story, reveal his true identity and teach us how to live fully human lives. During my defining life moments, I saw Jesus' divinity and humanity in a new way. I experienced the powerful presence of God. His teachings, miracles, death, and resurrection comforted me with the realization that his dying and rising continue in my life.

The Son of God became a man so that we might become like God. This "becoming God-like" constitutes our final destiny and our ultimate fulfillment as human beings. Jesus renews and reanimates humanity with the glory that humanity had before the Fall. Jesus renewed humanity through his life, suffering, and death on the cross. At the Last Supper, Jesus instituted the new covenant, and the Eucharist is its memorial and sign. In testimony to this covenant, God raised Jesus up to testify that he is the son of God.

The gospel stories illustrate God's invitation to conversion and repentance, prerequisites to the renewal of humankind. The story of the conversion of the good thief on the cross illustrates this well (Lk 23:39–43). This story is about a man who maintained a basic goodness in spite of his failings. He needed God's saving graces after leading a criminal life. He accepted these graces, but the other criminal, who hung next to him on the cross, mocked Jesus. The good thief rebuked this man's mockery and said,

> "Do you not fear God, since you are under the same sentence of condemnation? And we indeed have been condemned justly, for we are getting what we deserve for our deeds, but this man has done nothing wrong." Then he said, "Jesus, remember me when you come into your kingdom." He replied, "Truly I tell you, today you will be with me in Paradise." (Lk 23:40b–43).

Jesus' continual pattern of forgiveness and reconciliation offers us hope. We can be confident that he was tempted and suffered like us, and that he never ceases to invite us to return to him, no matter what we have done.

Another beautiful story illustrating Jesus' humanness and his desire to offer the sinner another chance is described in the story of the Samaritan woman at the well (Jn 4:1–42). By speaking to this woman and asking her for a drink of water, Jesus went beyond accepted Jewish norms in favor of the higher law of love. He wanted her conversion. He sensed her suffering. He reached out to her and offered her life-giving waters. Her answer, "give me this water so that I may never be thirsty" has been repeated by people throughout the ages who seek conversion and new life.

Jesus' stories can trigger memories of similar situations in our lives that call for compassion, forgiveness, endurance, patience, or common sense. Jesus' story and my Catholic faith help me appreciate what it means to be fully human and to find God's presence in my humanness and in the joy of helping others. While meditating on Jesus' story, I realized that being human means living according to God's designs. Cooperation with God's grace elevates ordinary actions, gives them dignity, and continues Jesus' mission of healing a broken world. My faith in Jesus helps me acknowledge that healing brings wholeness and that in wholeness I achieve my full humanity.

We announce Jesus' message of love to others through our teaching and inspire them through example. We become fully human to the degree that we become Christ-like. Paul says, "The gifts he gave were…for building up the body of Christ, until all of us come to the unity of the faith and the knowledge of the Son of God, to maturity, to the measure of the full stature of Christ" (Eph 4:11a, 13). Paul indicates that Jesus is the measuring rod against which we compare ourselves. Striving to become a complete man or woman depends on faith, not on intelligence, physical appearance, or talent. It is when we turn over our lives to God and invite Jesus to live within us that we can become fully human.

When we choose earthly rewards over God, we make ourselves the measure of all things. Sin inverts the order of the universe that God designed and leads to alienation and despair. Sin hinders us from discovering what it means to live in this world as God intended us to live. Turning back to God, however, is always possible. When we repent, alienation lessens and new hope begins. Because Jesus' story helps us live full human lives, we use his law of love to judge our lives.

The Theological Virtues in Jesus' Life

The Church describes virtues essential for a Christian life. The theological and cardinal moral virtues, illustrated in Jesus' life and teaching, disclose what it means to follow him. God infuses us with the three theological virtues—faith, hope, and love—to enable us to live as God's children and to merit entrance into eternal life.

Faith. Jesus' story teaches us the need for faith. Jesus had faith in his heavenly Father. He manifested his faith in the garden the night before he died when he cried out, "Yet, not my will but yours be done"(Lk 22:42b). Jesus, in turn, demanded faith from his followers. Jesus told his followers, "If you had faith the size of a mustard seed, you could say to this mulberry tree, 'Be uprooted and planted in the sea', and it would obey you"(Lk 17:6). The early Church, especially Paul, spoke of faith. For Paul, faith is the ultimate test of our commitment to God. When faith wanes Christians stray from God.

Faith in God leads to prayer. Jesus' whole life was a constant prayer of praise to his heavenly Father. Before important events Jesus went aside to pray, and he commanded his disciples to do the same: "Ask, and it will be given to you; search, and you will find; knock, and the door will be opened for you" (Mt 7:7). Without faith I do not know what I might have done during my sickness and when facing the death of my parents.

Hope. The hope of eternal life inspired the early Christians. The virtue of hope is manifested particularly in the Acts of the Apostles, the New Testament letters, and the Book of Revelation. For Paul, God is a "God of hope" (Rom 15:13). Hope rests on faith in God's promises (Rom 4:17–21). Hope brings with it confidence and unwavering trust. Hope and trust in times of suffering come not from human powers but from the gift of the Holy Spirit (Rom 5:4–5). Hope is given both to the Christian community as a whole and to individual disciples. Those who share new life in Christ are joined in hope.

During the deepest agony of my sickness and the profound grief that overcame me after my father and my mother died, the virtue of hope sustained me. I often thought, "Lord, if you could endure your pain for me, I have hope that your graces will sustain me."

Jesus trusted his Father when he turned his life over to the Father during his agony in the garden and death on Calvary. Jesus tells us to do the same: "Therefore I tell you, do not to worry about your life, what you will eat, or about your body, what you will wear....Do not be afraid, little flock, for it is your Father's good pleasure to give you the kingdom" (Lk 12:22, 32). Hope leads to confidence and trust in God.

Love. Jesus based his life on the Great Commandment of love, which is the key aspect of his story. Once a lawyer asked Jesus what he must do to inherit eternal life. Jesus responded by asking him, "What is written in the law?" (Lk 10:26). The lawyer responded, "You shall love the Lord your God with all your heart, and with all your soul, and with all your strength, and with all your mind; and your neighbor as yourself" (27). Jesus told the man to base his life on this commandment; he tells us to do the same.

Jesus illustrated this law of love throughout his life story in his teaching and his actions. In the story of the Good Samaritan, in the curing of the paralytic, in his reaction to Zaccheus and to the woman caught in adultery, Jesus puts love above the letter of the law. Many gospel stories invite us both to remember our stories and to gauge our reaction against Jesus' reaction.

Jesus' stories also are models around which to shape our future actions. Jesus constantly calls us to conversion. Jesus showed the depths of his love through his suffering and death on the cross. Just as he suffered because of love for us, we must show our love by sacrificing for one another. Through the centuries, martyrs and great saints give us profound examples of Christian love by their sacrifices.

Jesus' generosity extended to the gift of his life for us. Because of this gracious love we, too, are to be generous. Because Jesus was fully human, he struggled to love those who offended him. His actions give us the courage to look at our stories and celebrate the struggle to love as Jesus did.

As fully divine, Jesus loved us with infinite love. The Word who created us celebrates our love and grieves for our sins. Out of divine generosity, he redeemed us. His love goes beyond anything we can imagine. The internal unity of his divine and human natures was so complete that Jesus always chose to love. As his followers we strive for the same goal.

The Cardinal Virtues in Jesus' Story

The cardinal moral virtues are the virtues of prudence, justice, fortitude, and temperance. They are stable dispositions that direct our actions and conduct so that our conduct is in line with our faith and reason. We see them in Jesus' story.

Prudence. Fully human, Jesus had to choose to do the right thing. For example, he had to make a choice during his temptations in the desert, when he cured the man on the Sabbath, when he called the children to him, and when he went off by himself to pray. In all of these, he exercised the virtue of prudence. The virtue of prudence helps us discern what is right and good and what are the right means to accomplish this.

Just as prudence was an earmark of Jesus' life, it must be a central virtue in our lives. Without prudence, we go astray. In choosing a prudent action, we look to Jesus' example, invoke the Holy Spirit's help, and pray to the Father.

Justice. We are to love our neighbors and practice the virtue of justice. This demands that we give to God and our neighbor their due. Jesus stressed justice in his life and preached justice for those in need (Lk 6:20–23). Jesus identified with the downtrodden "just as you did it to one of the least of these who are members of my family, you did it to me" (Mt 25:40b).

Jesus' love and justice inspire us to Christian service. His life was one of humble service in the ordinary circumstances of daily living. He served the poor and neglected. This attitude of service inspires us to respond as Jesus did, by reaching out to our brothers and sisters. "Whoever wishes to be great among you must be your servant, and whoever wishes to be first among you must be your slave; just as the Son of Man came not to be served but to serve, and to give his life a ransom for many" (Mt 20:26b–28).

Fortitude. Fortitude or courage is a Christian badge of honor. We see this aspect of Jesus' story when we read his passion accounts. "They stripped him and put a scarlet robe on him, and after twisting some thorns into a crown, they put it on his head. They put a reed in his right hand..." (Mt 27:28–29a). We need the virtue of fortitude when temptation buffets us, sufferings beset us, or dread brings us to the limits of our endurance. When we face a crisis we can recall that Jesus endured a similar fate during his temptations in the desert and in his last hours.

Temperance. The virtue of temperance moderates our desire for pleasure and gives us the spiritual help to set a balance in the use of created things. Temperance can mean "good sense" or "sensible wisdom." In considering Jesus' story, we learn the importance of temperance, often manifested as self-control. Numerous references in the New Testament point to self-control as a key virtue in Jesus' teaching. In Paul's writings, self-control refers to discipline regarding sexual desires (1 Cor 7:9). Temperance requires the grace of the Holy Spirit.

When we pray, keeping in mind the elements of Jesus' story reflected in the theological and cardinal moral virtues, we are moved to humility. We see our insufficiencies and remember that being humble connects our lives with Jesus (Mt 18:14, 23:12). Humility is often used in the New Testament to describe the qualities of a faithful Christian. It shifts our foundation of authority from pride and position to our association with Jesus, and balances the human tendency to self-reliance.

Following Jesus to the Cross

Jesus promised that following him leads to eternal life. Mary, his mother, must have suffered greatly during Jesus' last hours, as did John, the beloved apostle. In John we read, "When Jesus saw his mother and the disciple whom he loved standing beside her, he said to his mother, 'Woman, here is your son.' Then he said to the disciple, 'Here is your mother'" (Jn 19:26–27).

Christian tradition teaches that after Jesus died, his body was placed in the arms of his mother. Michelangelo's famous sculpture, the Pietà, captures this tradition for posterity. We cannot fathom Mary's feelings, but the relationship of Jesus and his mother gleaned from New Testament accounts sheds some light on what she may have felt.

Mary had faith in God throughout her life, beginning with the Annunciation. Imagine how Jesus' death tested her faith when she saw him rejected, beaten, nailed to the cross, suffer for three hours, and die. Jesus, God's chosen one, was abandoned because of sin and thrown at her feet on a barren hill. As the ancient hymn says, "What sorrow is there like her sorrow?" Mary remained strong. She may have been tempted to despair, but never wavered. She suffered excruciating agony to give us a powerful reminder to place our absolute confidence in God.

I cannot describe what went on in me when I held my mother's hand after her death. The good times we shared flashed before me. At the cross Mary must have recalled the love she shared with Jesus. Did she not recall his first smile, family prayer, visits to relatives, his miracles, and the simple joy of being with Jesus? As Mary held her son did she wonder, as I did at my mother's bedside, "Why?" Did she ask over and over if it could have been otherwise, as I did? Did she not also cry?

The more I meditated on Mary's agony, the more I appreciated that my mother's death helped me understand what Mary endured at the cross. And I appreciated that Jesus' death helped me understand my mother's death. I saw how my story and Jesus' story complement each other. They are two sides of the same story: the story of God's love, human love, and the need for redemption. Such thoughts gave me hints about the anticipated fulfillment of our desire for God in heaven. Jesus' story gives meaning to the joys and sorrows present in my story.

Jesus' resurrection is the climax of his story. Our eventual resurrection will be the same. The God-man, who invites us to follow him, promises us eternal life. In our stories, we will experience the eventual realization of his story.

Revelation of the Trinity

The second defining aspect of Jesus' story is his revelation of God's story, the Trinity. The Trinity has played a vital role in my life, especially at key moments. In childhood I learned about Jesus and his Father in heaven. My mother and father taught me to love God and neighbor and to pray to the Holy Spirit for guidance. Jesus' presence in the Eucharist played a special role in my growing spirituality. This devotion continued through my adolescence and adult life.

During times of sickness, Jesus' image on the cross gave me courage. His resurrection brought me hope. When my father died, I felt an intimate bond between God the Father and my earthly father, especially when I prayed. I heard my father and God the Father's voice as if they were one. This experience of their voices happened many times. I remember the morning after my father died. As I was getting up, I heard my father's voice while I experienced God's presence. This voice said, "Bob, don't worry about me. I am with God."

When Mom was dying, a different manifestation of God occurred. As I prayed, I sensed the Holy Spirit's presence, giving me the wisdom to decide whether to insert a feeding tube to keep my mother alive. The Spirit directed me to seek advice from the hospital chaplain. This priest and I believed that the Spirit was moving us to conclude that no feeding tube should be inserted. When I discussed our reflections with Mom, she told me that she prayed all morning and received the same answer.

The Trinity Comes Alive

Jesus' teaching on the Trinity comes alive in core life events when believers connect these events with Jesus' teaching. Indeed, the things I learned during life's defining moments were enhanced when I related them to biblical events. Meditating on Jesus' teaching about his Father and the Spirit helped me appreciate the Trinity's presence in my life.

To fathom the role of the Trinity in our lives, it helps to reflect on the Last Supper in John's gospel. During this meal Jesus revealed the working of the Trinity: Father, Son, and Holy Spirit. A series of events form the backdrop of Jesus' discourse on the Father and Holy Spirit. These include Jesus' washing of the disciple's feet, his prediction of Judas' betrayal and Peter's denial, and his giving a new commandment. Couched within these powerful actions Jesus clearly indicates the actions of the Trinity.

When I think of Jesus reflecting on his final meal with his disciples, I wonder how a dying person must feel to realize that his or her children, spouse, brothers, or sisters are not reconciled with each other. In one family a conflict broke out between the children of a deceased woman after the wake service. These children had been at odds with each other while the woman was alive, and they were waiting for their last living parent to die so they could get the inheritance. Thank God that when my mother died, she knew that our family was unified and loving. We bent over backward to encourage each other to take whatever he or she wanted or needed from mom's possessions before we divided the rest. It was hard enough for our mother to leave us, even knowing that we were close to each other. What was it like for the mother of the greedy children? What was it like for their family?

Approaching Jesus' life and death from the vantage point of our experiences gives us a clue into what Jesus must have felt on different occasions. As his crucifixion approached, Jesus knew Judas would betray him and Peter would deny him in spite of his love for them. Was Jesus ever tempted to abandon his ungrateful disciples or ask himself if it was worth dying for them? The gospel tells us that the answer to this question is "no." Jesus' love for his disciples, even when they sinned, was so strong that he never stopped loving them. John says, "Having loved his own who were in the world, he loved them to the end" (Jn 13:1).

Jesus gives us great insights into the mystery of the Trinity within the context of the disciples' misunderstanding and betrayal. To show his love for them, he washed the disciples' feet (Jn 13:2–11). Jesus assumed the condition of a slave to teach them what God is like. When he finished washing their feet, Jesus told them, "You also ought to wash one another's feet" (Jn 13:14). Jesus then indicated that one of his disciples would betray him. He said that when it happens, "you may believe that I am he" (Jn 13:19). The latter phrase is direct reference to Jesus' divinity.

After Judas left the meal, Jesus told his disciples that his glory would be revealed and that God would be glorified through him. In spite of Judas' betrayal and Peter's denial, Jesus still calls his disciples "little children" (Jn 13:33). By calling the disciples "children" Jesus says something profound about God, especially when Jesus adds, "I give you a new commandment, that you love one another" (Jn 13:34). These words remind me of the deep love that parents often feel for their children. They love their children regardless of what the children have done.

The servant dimension of Jesus' story prepares us for his teaching on the way we must take to go to the Father. This way consists in living the law of love. The disciples had to believe and act as Jesus did if they hoped to know the Father. "Whoever has seen me has seen the Father" (Jn 14:9). Jesus refers to his relationship with the Father and the Holy Spirit during his farewell discourse at the Last Supper. He says, "I am in the Father and the Father is in me" (Jn 14:10).

After Jesus announced that he would leave his followers, he sensed their distress and encouraged them to remember what he had taught them. His words, "Whoever has seen me has seen the Father" (Jn 14:9) reveal the Father's love and compassion. Our love for Jesus is connected with the Father's love of us. Jesus says, "Those who love me will keep my word, and my Father will love them, and we will come to them and make our home with them" (Jn 14:23). These words reveal the close bonds between Jesus and his Father.

As the discourse continues, Jesus next refers to the Holy Spirit, the third person of the Trinity. He tells his disciples that "the Advocate, the Holy Spirit, whom the Father will send in my name, will teach you everything" (Jn 14:26). He promises the Holy Spirit to those who believe in him and obey his commandments (Jn 15:10–16). Finally, Jesus speaks of the Holy Spirit and says, "This is the Spirit of truth, whom the world cannot receive, because it neither sees him nor knows him. You know him, because he abides with you, and he will be in you" (Jn 14:17).

During his final words with the disciples, Jesus showed the depths of God's love by giving them his body and blood to eat and drink. This testimony of love was the final gift of a savior who continued to love, despite his disciples' betrayal. When Jesus' last meal was completed, he prepared for his death, a death that liberated us from the effects of Adam's sin. From the beginning of biblical history, the Jews anticipated their liberation from sin and oppression. Biblical stories tell of God's revelation through prophets, kings, patriarchs, and wise people. When the time to fulfill the messianic hope arrived, Jesus showed the depths of God's love through his suffering, death, and resurrection.

We cannot grasp this Trinitarian story by reason alone. Jesus alone reveals this mystery, hidden in God. Jesus teaches us enough about the Father and the Spirit for us to believe, worship, thank, and love the Triune God who gives us life.

Jesus' revelation enabled the Church, including the Church Fathers and other theologians, to probe this mystery. The Church's basic belief includes the belief that there are three distinct divine persons in the Trinity, namely, the Father, Son, and Holy Spirit. These three persons have one divine nature.

Sharing the Life of the Trinity

Our unfulfilled yearnings and feelings of incompleteness make sense only in light of the God who made us, loves us, and desires that we live in divine friendship forever. Human aspirations reach fulfillment only in the Trinity.

Jesus tells us that becoming fully human and reaching our fulfillment in life means accepting the salvation won by Jesus' life, death, and resurrection. This salvation is brought about through the workings of the Trinity and the activities of the Church. We receive everything we are and have from our Triune God who gives us life. God continues to share these graces through the Church.

Life is God's free gift, and the new life received through grace is God's special gift. This grace is rooted in God's relationship with us and our relationship with God, the Church, and one another. After Adam and Eve's sin God did not abandon us. Neither does God abandon us after we sin. The Father calls us back, the Son shows us the way, and the Holy Spirit moves us to sin no more.

God's life within us influences our relationships with others. Recognizing my need for other people during my sickness and at both my father's and mother's death helped me appreciate that we are saved in community, not in isolation. Salvation begins in the immanent operations of the Trinity, is revealed in the Scripture, is accomplished in Jesus' dying and rising, and comes to us through the Church.

As a child, I learned that I need others. I learned to do good and avoid evil. I learned these things through my parents' love and our family's respect for God, one another, and the Church. The good example of teachers and classmates at St. William's School reinforced this understanding. My faith, and the accompanying virtues associated with it, was strengthened at Elder High School. Everything about me—home, relatives, friends, neighbors, and schools—reinforced my Catholic identity.

Through such positive experiences, honed in a communal setting, I learned about God's love. In the course of growing up, I met people who were not attuned to God's love. In such encounters, I sensed the evil of sin. Sifting out the good from the bad was not easy for me as a child, teenager, and young adult. Through it all, I discovered that God never works in a vacuum; we are saved or lost in community. I came to this from my life story, from the stories of those around me, through prayer, through God's word, through Jesus' story, and through Church teachings.

The Body of Christ: The Church

Jesus' call of the disciples, especially Peter and the apostles, set the stage for the third defining dimension in his life, namely establishing the foundation for the Church, the Body of Christ.

The disciples' call took a profound turn during his suffering and death. Until the passion, they followed him, accepted his preaching, and hoped he was the anticipated messiah. His agony and crucifixion were turning points for them—most ran away. Saints, bishops, and theologians have said that the Church was born when the soldier pierced Jesus' side and blood and water flowed. In other words, the Church was born out of pain and suffering.

We cannot understand the Church without connecting it with Christ's suffering and death, the sacrifice of Christian martyrs, and the courageous deaths of Jesus' faithful followers of every generation. Christians who are faithful to the end of their lives win Jesus' salvation and the benefits bestowed upon a suffering yet glorious Church.

Christians do not always understand why they suffer. Neither did Jesus. In the garden Jesus asked the Father to remove his cup of suffering, if it was his Father's will (Lk 22:41–42). Many faithful followers of Jesus ask the same thing. Jesus died alone, except for his mother, a few disciples, the thieves, and soldiers. Those present who loved him symbolize the faithful Church that was born into its full glory at Pentecost. Believers never die alone. Even if no other human being is present, the Triune God is with them. So are Mary, Mary Magdalene, John, and a chorus of angels and saints. The communion of saints supports them as they breathe their last and enter eternal life.

As social animals, we require support beyond money, food, and shelter. We have to give and receive love during times of joy, celebration, hurt, pain, and death. We need community support. Jesus gave us his Church, the people of God, to support us spiritually. Without the Church we would not be assured of God's love and our worth as God's children. The Body of Christ, especially expressed in our families and loved ones, discloses God's loving presence. I depend on the support of family and close friends, as well as the prayers and help of the broader Church community. They show me God's loving presence during good and difficult times.

Unfortunately we occasionally lack the support of the Church community. Jesus experienced the same thing. Some of his friends failed to support him in his greatest need. Despite his lack of support, he remained faithful, was true to what was right, and condemned evil. His actions offer us a powerful example when we experience a lack of support from the Church.

During my defining life moments, most hospital chaplains and nursing home personnel reflected God's love. The dedication of these ministers made Jesus' presence in the sacraments more apparent to me, especially in communion, at Mass, and during the anointing of the sick. I experienced in them the living witness of Jesus' promise to love us, remain with us always, and give eternal life to God's faithful people.

Jesus entrusted the Church with the responsibility of preserving the spirit of love and the truth revealed through Scripture. The Christian community continues this preservation through its witness, the teaching of its basic beliefs, liturgical celebrations, service ministry, and parish life. As one convert put it, "People are drawn into the Church through their experience of God's love in the form of service, Christian community, and the liturgy."

The Church's basic beliefs, centered on the Great Commandment to love, console us during times of sickness and death. We cannot achieve our final goal of eternal happiness by ourselves, but only through the gifts bestowed upon us by our Triune God. Jesus offers us God's blessings, which reach their fulfillment in heaven. As a special gift to us, Jesus gave us his Church, where he continues his love through the ministry of God's faithful people.

II. A Response to God's Love

Jesus came so that we might be freed from sin, sickness, and death. Jesus' response to hurting people illustrates God's desire that we be whole and happy. Jesus bound up people's wounds, shared his possessions, gave hungry people loaves and fish in the desert, and offered his disciples the Eucharist at the Last Supper. Our stories mirror his story when we serve the needy and celebrate the Eucharist. Jesus' story invites us to live and love as he did, to become God-like.

Laurie, a college student, told a story that illustrates how she responded to Jesus' call.

> Not long after I made my First Communion, my family spent a weekend in a large city. We stayed in a motel in the downtown area. On the second evening there my family decided to eat dinner in our hotel room. Dad called in an order of sandwiches, pizzas, and drinks to a local carry-out store. Soon, a deliveryman knocked on our door and gave us the food. We gathered for dinner around the table near a window two stories above the street.
>
> As I opened my sandwich and Mom cut the pizzas, I looked out the window and saw a homeless man on the street, rooting though a garbage can for food. He ate what he found. I looked at the tasty food before me and thought of my First Communion. I told my Dad that I wanted to give the man my sandwich and pizza. I asked him to bring me downstairs in order to give him my dinner.
>
> My Dad replied, "That's generous of you, Laurie. If you do this, we'll give you some of our food." Soon, Dad and I were outside on the sidewalk. I gave the food to the man and he thanked me. Returning upstairs, I was anxious to watch the man eat my dinner, while I ate some food provided by my family.
>
> I noticed that the man did not immediately eat the food. Instead, he walked around the block and invited two other homeless people to join him. When they were together, they bowed their heads to give thanks. Then he shared my food with them. I was moved, knowing that he must have been very hungry, since he was eating garbage. He could have eaten all the food I gave him. Seeing him share the food made me happy. I not only shared my food with him, but he also shared his food with other needy people.

As a small child, Laurie learned to be God-like through the good example of her family and the excellent instructions she received before her First Communion. She read her children's Bible, and learned how Jesus shared his life. Laurie learned to do the same. As an adult Laurie said, "It's so easy to do something that really makes a difference. We just have to recognize such times when they arise."

We cannot become God-like by ourselves. We need the larger faith community to show us the way. This guidance usually begins with our families. Even more than guidance, we need God's grace, which elevates us to a new life in Christ. The Christian community is a means that God uses to give us the gift of grace. We can become God-like because Jesus became one of us, because he showed us the way through his story, and because he left us the Church to guide us.

III. Jesus' Story Celebrated

When my mother celebrated her seventy-fifth birthday, the family had a surprise party for her. She arrived at my brother's house, saw her family and friends, and was dumfounded. Responding like a youngster, Mom said, "This is the first time anyone has ever had a surprise party for me." It was a special celebration of our love that she never forgot.

Celebrations manifest human love. They also celebrate our love for God. Religious celebrations, like Christmas, Easter, a baptism, and the Eucharist, ritualize our deepest beliefs. They acknowledge who we are, where we came from, what our destiny is, and how we are to live our life. They celebrate our response to God's love by honoring and worshiping God.

In Christian celebrations we worship God as our creator and redeemer. Such celebrations begin in baptism, when we commit ourselves to follow Jesus' way. They continue in the other sacraments, especially the Eucharist, when we profess the unique presence of the Son of God who redeemed us.

The activity of the Father, Son, and Holy Spirit invites us to become fully human by worshiping and by cooperating with God's graces. This worship reaches its highest point in eucharistic celebrations. When worshiping God at Mass, we profess our faith in the Father as creator, the Son as redeemer, and the Holy Spirit as sanctifier. At Mass we acknowledge our humanity, affirm our dignity, and solidify our earthly role as the people of God.

Jesus' story was revealed to us through the early Christian community, as it sifted through his words and actions and put down the truths he conveyed in words under the inspiration of the Holy Spirit. Their writings are found in the New Testament. Chapter Four looks at how Jesus followers have incorporated key aspects of his story into their basic beliefs and practices.

Points for Reflection

- What experiences in your life have disclosed God's presence? How do these experiences affect your attitude toward others?

- What would you name as defining moments in Jesus' story? Why? Which connect with your story?

- If you could ask Jesus to name the important defining moments in his story, what do you think he would say?

- What implications do the defining moments from Jesus' life that you mentioned above have for your relationship with family members? For actions in your professional life?

- What do you regard as the most important qualities or virtues that Jesus' story reveals? For example, love, gratitude, or generosity? Which of these qualities do you find in your life? in your family? in your parish? Which qualities do you need to develop more fully?

- Have you ever asked, "Why?" when facing with a tragedy? How can Jesus' story help you during such times?

- In your everyday life, does the promise of an eternal reward after this earthly life motivate you to do good and avoid evil? Why or why not?

- Has the Church supported you in times of need? Give an example. Then give instances when family or friends supported you. How did their support compare with that of the Church?

- Give examples of people who are God-like in their life and actions. Would you put yourself in this list? Why or why not?

- If you asked your family and friends, would they say that you reflect Jesus' message of love and forgiveness?

- "We cannot become God-like by ourselves. We need the larger faith community to show us the way." Why?

- Which stories from your life do the stories in this chapter bring to mind?

- What is the most important insight that you gleaned from this chapter? Why does it have special significance? What does it tell you about your life?

Biblical Passages for Reflection

- Since God has forgiven us, we are to forgive others. Reflect on Luke's words, "Father, forgive them; for they do not know what they are doing" (Lk 23:34). Apply these words to a situation in which a person hurt you. Reflect on how Jesus' words can be a pattern for your future behavior when you are offended.

- Reflect on Romans 4:17–21, which speaks of hope. Ask God for wisdom in times when you are losing hope. Remember Paul's words that hope rests on God's promise.

- Read the passion account in Matthew's gospel (Mt 26–28) in light of the courage demanded in painful situations or in difficult decisions.

Action Steps

Lessons learned. Discuss with a family member, friend, or pastoral minister the lessons learned from the story of the

Siberian people or from the story of the girl who gave her food to the homeless man. How are such stories like sermons? What similar stories exist in your life?

Family discussion. Invite family members to discuss how they can better respond to the needy in the neighborhood or in the city. Use Advent or Lent as times to meet and discuss how to become involved in social justice issues.

Support the elderly. Sometimes it is easy to forget that frail adults are fully human. Identify a person or persons from your family, friends, or neighborhood who live at home or in a retirement home. Visit them on a regular basis and encourage them to tell their stories. Affirm the contributions they continue to make to life. Pray with them and ask for their blessing before you leave. Make this a regular practice. If you do not know anyone to visit, ask your parish pastoral minister for the name of a person.

Express gratitude. At Thanksgiving or another family gathering, have each family member identify a person present at the gathering for whom he or she wishes to give thanks. (A name could be drawn out of a hat.) Then ask each person to say something nice about the individual and agree to pray for him or her in the future. Make sure that no one is left out.

Read a book on justice. Get a copy of John Paul II's book, *Church in America* (*Ecclesia in America,* Washington, DC: United States Catholic Conference, 1999) or a similar book, and read it. Concentrate on books that center on ministry to the poor. Discuss what you have learned with a friend, work colleague, or parish member.

Chapter Four

Defining Periods in the Church's Story

"I am the way, and the truth, and the life.
No one comes to the Father except through me." (Jn 14:6)

Jesus' story was revealed to us through the early Christian community. The community sifted through his words and actions and compiled the truths he conveyed under the inspiration of the Holy Spirit. These truths are found in the New Testament. This chapter looks at how Jesus' followers incorporated key aspects of his story into their basic beliefs and practices.

There is a story in missionary history that puts the verse above from John into clear focus. An anthropologist-preacher named Jacob recounted it. (If any reader knows the origin of this story, please contact me so that I can thank the writer. I do not know where I first read this story.)

Coming to God

For two years the anthropologist-preacher Jacob studied the native language of the tribe he hoped to evangelize. When he felt prepared, he left by ship and landed on the distant coast where the native people lived. Jacob was eager to teach them about God's love. Initially the people regarded this white-skinned foreigner as an oddity. Curious to learn why he came, the natives listened to his message. Jacob told them about the Christian God. He narrated the story of Jesus' passion, death, and resurrection and said that Jesus gave his life for them. They laughed spontaneously. Stunned at their response, he soon discovered why they rejected Jesus and refused to listen to his teaching on the Great Commandment.

These people found humor in Jesus' message of mercy and forgiveness because they regarded these virtues as signs of weakness. Their greatest virtue was deceit, and therefore Judas was their hero. Judas was clever enough to worm his way into Jesus' select disciples in order to deceive and betray him. Jacob tried to explain, but the people kept laughing at his efforts to preach Jesus' message of forgiveness.

Frustrated and disappointed, Jacob planned to leave the people. Curiously the tribe, especially the chief, liked Jacob. When he announced his departure, everyone begged him to stay. Jacob declined their request. During his time with them, he witnessed many wars with neighboring tribes. Some even took place near his hut. Jacob did not want to stay.

In one final effort to encourage Jacob to stay, the chief assembled his tribe before Jacob's hut. The chief also invited the tribe with whom they were most frequently at war. When all were assembled, the chief took his six-month-old son from his sobbing wife's arms and offered him to the other chief. The other chief accepted the baby boy. In so doing, this chief pledged to raise the child as his own. The baby would become a full member of his tribe and would take the chief's name. According to their custom, a child given in this way was a "peace child," and as long as the peace child lived, war was forbidden between the two tribes.

After observing this ritual, Jacob was upset. The patriarchal nature of the story bothered him. Two male chiefs decided to take a child from his mother as a solution to war. At the same time, Jacob saw this gesture as an opportunity to lead the tribe to the Christian way. Jacob used their primitive practice as a starting point to move them to freedom and salvation in Christ.

Jacob preached one final sermon. Jacob described Jesus as the divine peace child and God's Son. Jacob explained that Jesus' Father gave him up to atone for sin. He told them that this divine peace child became one of us and reconciled us with God. Now, Jacob said, there can be peace on earth because his Father gave us his only Son. Jacob explained that Jesus came among his enemies and brought peace. Jacob assured the tribe that it was no longer necessary for one chief to give up a son to bring peace because Jesus sacrificed for all of us.

After hearing Jacob's sermon, the tribe began to appreciate Jesus' story. They ended their warring ways, changed their philosophy of deceit, and accepted Jesus' teaching on the Great Commandment—his message of love, mercy, and forgiveness. Jacob stayed with the people for many years.

Throughout history, Christians have told the story of the divine peace child to various tribes and nations. Each interpreted it differently, depending on the time, place, people, and community. Jesus' story has interfaced with many cultures. Throughout time, basic Christian beliefs gleaned from Jesus' story have guided the Church.

The Relationship of Story and Belief

The story of Jacob and the tribe suggests essential components in the relationship between story and basic belief. They include the interplay of basic belief and story, the influence of culture, the role of the community, and the solidification of doctrine and its reformulation. Regardless of which form the story and belief take, they each must be rooted in Jesus' teaching on love and forgiveness.

The Catholic faith begins in the Christian story as revealed in Scripture and handed down through Catholic Tradition. We cannot understand our basic beliefs apart from Jesus' story of love. Neither can we teach effectively if we do not know Jesus' story or the basic beliefs that it contains. Jesus' story of God's love lays the foundation for doctrine and creed.

What is the relationship of story and basic belief? What two essential principles relate story and belief? How do we refocus our stories and basic belief?

Defining Periods in Church History

I have chosen to analyze these defining periods in Church history: early Christianity; heresy and the living Tradition; the Fathers of the Church; scholasticism; the Council of Trent; and Vatican II and the years following. These have been selected because each period brought about significant clarification of Church teaching and shifts in Church life, as well as insights into the relationship between the Church and society.

Early Christianity

After Pentecost, the Church proclaimed Jesus' coming and boldly spoke of his death and resurrection. Love, not knowledge, motivates Christian disciples. Early Christians lived in common, shared their possessions, and had "the goodwill of all the people" (Acts 2:47). "With great power the apostles gave their testimony to the resurrection of the Lord Jesus, and great grace was upon them all" (Acts 4:33). Christians faced many challenges. To address some of them, the community selected deacons to serve the needs of the poor and to distribute food to widows. The disciples faced persecution. Stephen was stoned, and some disciples initially found it hard to believe in Paul's conversion. During this entire time, early followers of Jesus framed what was happening to them within the context of Jesus' story.

Disagreements arose as the Church sifted out the theological implications of Jesus' story. For example, the first Christians wondered whether Gentile converts had to observe Jewish dietary laws and whether these converts had to be circumcised. In Chapter 15 of Acts of the Apostles, Peter addresses a meeting in Jerusalem (sometimes called the Council of Jerusalem). Peter argues against circumcision for pagans and against requiring them to follow the Law of

Moses. "We believe that we will be saved through the grace of the Lord Jesus, just as they will" (Acts 15:11). James then declared, "I have reached the decision that we should not trouble those Gentiles who are turning to God, but we should write to them to abstain only from things polluted by idols and from fornication and from whatever has been strangled and from blood" (Acts 15:19–20). This decision was made with knowledge of Jesus' practice and teaching. Acts of the Apostles points out the need to base Christian beliefs on Jesus' story and to remain faithful to his teachings.

Basic Christian beliefs flow from Jesus' story and the Church's living Tradition. The Catholic community acknowledges the special role of Peter and of the apostles and their successors in authenticating Catholic belief. Connecting Jesus' story with people's lives, with their ethnic heritage, and their religious culture is also important.

The Church began with a love story of Jesus who died and was raised up by his Father to save us from our sins, not with a set of basic beliefs. Inflamed by his love, early Christian leaders sifted out basic beliefs from his story. In the very beginning of this process, Peter had the final say, as we know from the New Testament and from the writings of Clement of Rome and Ignatius of Antioch.

As long as the first apostles were alive and Jesus' followers believed in his immanent return, the Church maintained clear expressions of Jesus' teachings. When the expectation of his return faded and Jesus' original followers died, the Church had to make a new effort to remember God's great love and to remain faithful to Jesus' teachings. This effort was especially needed when false teachings threatened to tear the Christian community asunder.

Heresy and the Living Tradition

A heresy known as Gnosticism arose in the Church near the end of the first century. The Gnostic movement illustrates how the Church clarified its belief in response to this false teaching. Gnostics claimed that Jesus was not really a man and that his human appearance was like a costume, concealing his true divinity.

Jesus only seemed to dwell in a human body. The Church condemned Gnosticism. If Gnosticism was true, Jesus could not redeem us from Adam's sin. For it took a real man (Jesus, the second Adam) to redeem the human race from the sin of the first man (the first Adam).

The pastoral epistles and the letters of Ignatius of Antioch were written in the shadow of the Gnostic movement. They describe Church governance under the bishops' authority at the end of the first century. To prevent the Church from breaking apart, the bishops assumed a unifying role and spoke authoritatively about basic beliefs. The need to keep the community intact in the face of the Gnostic challenge hastened the solidification of Church authority under them. Their authority was centralized in the pope, the bishop of Rome.

Erroneous teachings like Gnosticism helped the Christian community sift out the core elements of Jesus' story and unify them into basic Church beliefs. In the first century, many texts surfaced that claimed to be authentic sayings of Jesus. The Church accepted some of these texts and rejected others. The living Tradition that came from the apostles was the key factor in discerning a text's authenticity. The special role of the episcopacy in authenticating basic belief and practice was established. The role of the bishops in authenticating belief continues today. A pastoral perspective in theology, evidenced in the writings of the Fathers and Doctors of the Church, forms the backdrop for the Church's discernment of its basic belief. This pastoral approach centers on the Great Commandment of love.

Fathers of the Church: Athanasius and Augustine

Jesus' story reveals the Trinity, a foundational truth of Christianity. In the fourth century Arius challenged his bishop, Athanasius, over the relationship of the Father and the Son. Arius taught that Jesus had a beginning and could change. He denied Jesus' divinity and equality with the Father. To meet Arius' challenge, Emperor

Constantine called the Church's first ecumenical council at Nicea in 325 AD. The assembled bishops, many with little formal theological expertise, relied on the Christian Tradition to help them discern the truth.

The bishops condemned Arius' teaching that Jesus was created and that Jesus is not "identical in substance" with the Father. Even after this pronouncement, the controversy over Jesus' relationship with the Father continued. The Council of Constantinople (381 AD) affirmed the equality of the Three Persons, thus solidifying the Church's belief in the Trinity.

The theology that underlies the relationship of God the Father, the Son, and the Holy Spirit is based on Jesus' story. Church history makes it clear that Jesus' story grounds theological speculation. When someone like Arius moves too far away from the story itself, theological conclusions can become erroneous. The same principle applies to moral and pastoral issues. We cannot arrive at sound pastoral conclusions unless our stories interface with Jesus' story and the Church's story.

Early Church Fathers like Augustine, Basil, and Chrysostom provide models for subsequent theological inquiry. As pastors themselves, they took their pastoral experiences into account when drawing theological conclusions. They took seriously Jesus' injunction to love God and treat all men and women as brothers and sisters.

Augustine shows a pastoral orientation in the way he relates Scripture and basic beliefs to the challenges of his time. Augustine grew up in a Christian home, and St. Monica was his mother. Before his conversion Augustine lived a very worldly life and was a professor of rhetoric in Carthage and Rome. Becoming unsettled as the years passed, he returned to the teachings of his faith that he had learned in his youth. He began to read the Bible and to attend cathedral services in Milan. While listening to St. Ambrose preach there, his conversion intensified. He heard Jesus' message of true love, and Ambrose baptized him in 387 AD.

After his baptism Augustine lived a quasi-monastic life at Hippo in Africa. Bishop Valerius ordained him and eventually appointed him as co-adjutor bishop in 395 AD. When Valerius died Augustine became bishop of Hippo. Augustine's previous worldly lifestyle and his concern for his people influenced his theology. Love of God, pastoral zeal, and commitment to the truth led him to oppose heresy. He became embroiled in many theological controversies. His desire to address pastoral needs in his diocese and in the broader Church caused him, many times, to interrupt the writing of his classic work on the Trinity.

Augustine taught a narrow view of human freedom in relation to God's grace. Even though he is called the "Doctor of Grace," some of his teachings contain theological elements that later Church councils found incompatible with Jesus' story and the Church's Tradition.

No single theologian is the final arbiter of the Church's basic beliefs. The Church depends on Scripture, especially Jesus' story, and its living Tradition to determine what is true. Augustine's story can encourage theologians and pastoral ministers to work toward new and better ways to express basic belief and practice and to search for insights into the Holy Spirit's activity today.

Scholasticism and the Council of Trent

The Middle Ages marked a shift in the relationship between story and basic belief. During this time, scholasticism—a systematic approach to theology exemplified in the work of Thomas Aquinas—flourished, and great theological syntheses developed. These syntheses set the stage for the more formal doctrinal approach used at the Council of Trent (1545–1563), a council that influenced Catholic life until the Second Vatican Council (1962–1965).

Universities, like those in Paris and Padua, were centers of scholarship. Monks poured over ancient tomes, and new translations of Aristotle's writings inspired theologians like Albert, Thomas, Bonaventure, Scotus, and Suarez. Theologians developed syntheses of Catholic teaching. Thomas Aquinas' *Summa Theologica*, a synthesis of Catholic teaching, was based on Scripture, the Church Fathers, and Aristotle's philosophical writings. During the medieval period, reason predominated and academic theologians assumed a new role.

Controversies and debates developed between theologians over certain beliefs about grace, human freedom, and providence. These debates often became quite speculative, for example, the controversy surrounding God's grace and human freedom. Some medieval theologians had less pastoral contact with the believing community than the Fathers of the Church had. Some medieval theology centered more on the intricacies of basic belief than on Jesus' story.

During the thirteenth and fourteenth centuries, the Church also grew through the witness of holy people, like Francis of Assisi, Dominic, and Clare, who kept Jesus' story in the forefront. The saints lived the Great Commandment. Their theology influenced their pastoral practice, while their pastoral practice shed new insights on their theology. Through them, Jesus' story inspired and inspires Church members to be witnesses to God's Word.

When the Church neglects Jesus' story, distortions occur. Forgiveness, compassion, and love may no longer be the basis for Church life and practice. The terrible atrocities committed against the Jews in the Middle Ages indicate how far the Church drifted from the message of the gospels.

Failing to live by Jesus' story, especially his command to love God and neighbor, has produced dire consequences in the life of the Church. I learned about these consequences when I asked Jake, an Amish builder, to construct my house in Indiana. We became friends as he and his three sons worked on the house. He invited me into his home and described his family rituals and religious practices. Once Jake asked me what I did for a living. I told him I was a teacher, but did not say that I was a Catholic priest. (On an earlier occasion, I had told another Amish man that I was a

Catholic. He replied, "Your ancestors persecuted my ancestors and burned our founder at the stake.")

The Anabaptists were spiritual ancestors of the Amish. They believed in rebaptism of those baptized in infancy. Catholics failed to heed Jesus' teaching on love of neighbor in regard to them. In the sixteenth century Catholics hunted down and killed Anabaptists. Jake knows this history. Just as Catholics honor their saints, the Amish honor their martyrs and saints, whose stories they read from their Book of Martyrs during religious services.

Someday I will tell Jake that I am a priest, and I will apologize for the Catholics who committed such horrible deeds against his ancestors. These Catholics had forgotten the meaning of Jesus' story. The histories of persecuted peoples remind us as individuals and as Church to keep Jesus' story in the forefront, lest basic beliefs and practices are distorted through power, arrogance, greed, or exaggerated rationalism.

The Effects of the Council of Trent

In the fifteenth and early-sixteenth centuries, the Church did not adequately address its serious problems. Unworthy popes and bishops, political corruption, distorted theology, and the abuse of power highlighted the need for reform. If Augustine's model of a pastoral bishop had been followed, the story of the late Middle Ages (including the Protestant Reformation), may have been different.

When Luther hung his ninety-five theses on the door of the Wittenburg Cathedral in 1517, his action and subsequent events moved the Catholic Church to change. In reaction to the call for reform, the Catholic Church first responded defensively. As time went on, the Church recognized the need to set new directions, and it did so in the decrees of the Council of Trent. Its reforms largely followed the scholastic model, especially the work of Thomas Aquinas. His *Summa Theologica*, often in watered-down form, became the "bible" for subsequent Catholic theology from this council until the Second Vatican Council.

Reacting to the Protestant reformers, the Church at Trent stressed its authority and the centrality of the Eucharist in Catholic life. It also discouraged Catholics from reading the Bible as a means of spiritual growth, while emphasizing the importance of Church teachings. Although it effected important pastoral reforms, Trent's approach was strongly academic and rational in tone. After Trent, seminaries stressed Christ's divinity and often neglected his humanity. Scripture became a tool of apologetics used to prove that the Catholic Church is the one, true Church of Jesus Christ.

Following the Council of Trent, the Catholic Church often isolated itself from Jews, Protestants, and other religions. The Catholic community became a quasi-closed society insulated from the world's challenges. Theology, a special prerogative of the clergy, justified Church teaching and opposed Protestant beliefs. Cultural and ethnic perspectives within the Church received little attention. Seminarians learned basic Catholic teaching from manuals and rarely discussed the connection of Jesus' story and their stories as focal points of theology.

Sensing the sterility of this approach, bishops and pastors devised ways to connect Jesus' story with people's lives. One attempt is evident in the old *Third Reader*, published in 1881 by Benziger Brothers. The cover describes it as "thoroughly Catholic." The book contains stories that illustrate Catholic belief. This reader focused on Jesus' story and related to the grade level of the children. Other Catholic books like this reader taught children the Catholic faith in a holistic way.

The *Third Reader* was published nine years before the *Baltimore Catechism*. This catechism became the chief catechetical tool for instructing children, youth, and adults in the Catholic faith. It employed a rational, abstract approach, which followed the teachings of the *Catechism of the Council of Trent*, published in 1567. While solid in content, the *Baltimore Catechism* did not connect directly with people's lives.

In the years immediately preceding Vatican II, the Catholic Church grew and flourished. Seminarians, priests, and religious communities abounded. Parishes and Catholic schools increased in numbers. The Church emphasized devotions to the saints and published Catholic biographies, novels, and magazines for children and adults. The future looked bright.

Vatican II and Beyond

During the second half of the twentieth century something new was in the air. Society was changing, and the Church needed to update; Pope John XXIII called the Second Vatican Council (1962–1965).

A shift in theology and in pastoral practice was needed to meet the challenges of modern society. This contemporary shift began with this council. The council advocated a holistic approach to the human person, to community, to culture, and to ministry based on Jesus' story and his teaching on the Great Commandment. New interest developed in anthropology, history, psychology, sociology, and modern science. The council was concerned about the issues facing the Church in the modern world, including personal responsibility and human freedom.

The *Constitution on the Sacred Liturgy* revitalized the liturgy. It restored the catechumenate, which led to the Rite of Christian Initiation of Adults. The *Dogmatic Constitution on the Church* and the *Pastoral Constitution on the Church in the Modern World* addressed the Church as mystery and as the people of God. These documents recognized God's presence in society, in the Jewish faith, in other Christian denominations, and in world religions.

The *Dogmatic Constitution on Divine Revelation* emphasized Jesus' story and focused on the importance of learning and loving Scripture. Catholics were called to appreciate God's Word as the foundation for theology, spirituality, and liturgy. This document invited theologians to focus on Jesus' story and to show how it continues in the living witness of the Christian community.

As a result of Vatican II, Jesus' story, the Church's story, ethnic and social stories, and personal stories now underlie current theological speculation and pastoral practice. The other council's decrees also have a pastoral flavor; they also refocused the Church's basic beliefs and practices.

Council teachings changed the Catholic community's perspective on the global Church. Liturgical renewal affirmed inculturation, and liturgical texts were translated into vernacular languages. Missionaries began to look more intently on how Jesus' story connects with God's dealings with various tribes and peoples. Openness set the stage for a new evangelization and a better appreciation of how Third World countries can offer insights to the entire Church community.

The Church Today

A good balance is emerging between story and basic belief in the third millennium. The publication of the *Catechism of the Catholic Church* (1994), the *General Directory for Catechesis* (1997), and the *National Directory for Catechesis* (2005) helped balance the relationship between Jesus' story, our stories, and basic beliefs. We understand that Jesus' saving mission continues in our stories, especially in family life and at work.

Since stories are central to life, pastoral ministry and theology look to Jesus' use of story. By looking at stories, we return to a way of theologizing and ministering that was present in the New Testament. This return to stories requires a conviction about their importance and the skills necessary to reflect on them. Recognition that Jesus calls us to salvation by different paths helps pastoral leaders, parents, friends, and colleagues to be more open to various ways that sincere people find God.

The Relationship of Story and Belief

In reflecting on the history of the Christian community, two principles need to be considered when thinking about the relationship between the Christian story and basic beliefs. The first principle is that basic beliefs begin with stories. The second is that a story begins with experience.

Basic beliefs begin with stories. The Church's basic beliefs emerge from the Jewish and the Christian stories. These stories reveal God's presence in history and the covenant of love made with God's people. Doctrine, if seen only in the abstract, fails to recognize that revelation occurs in the context of this story and in the context of the entire human story. Teaching basic beliefs without linking them to Jesus' story fails to ground faith in the living story, a story that begins with the Jewish people and is brought to fulfillment in Jesus. The early Christian community first formulated the basic beliefs, and these beliefs have been reformulated in succeeding generations.

An *Informative Dossier,* published before the *Catechism of the Catholic Church,* clarifies the role of basic belief. It says, "In the New Testament, the Gospels are the first great 'Catechism' which was transmitted orally and then put into writing" (p. 11). In other words, the early Christian community derived the content of their belief and their behavior from Jesus. They looked to his message of God's love and his way of acting, preaching, and celebrating. The evangelists summarized the heart of his message in the Great Commandment, which is the lifeblood of Christianity.

Basic Catholic beliefs also come from Jesus' teachings on the kingdom of God. The apostles, first disciples, and early community leaders preserved Jesus' teachings complete and intact. In Matthew's gospel Jesus tells his followers to make disciples, "teaching them to obey everything that I have commanded you. And remember, I am with you always, to the end of the age" (Mt 28:20).

The *Catechism of the Catholic Church* says,

> The transmission of the Christian faith consists primarily in proclaiming Jesus Christ in order to lead others to faith in him. From the beginning, the first disciples burned with the desire to proclaim Christ: "We cannot but speak of what we have seen and heard." And they invited people of every era to enter into the joy of their communion with Christ. (425)

The Church of every generation centers its teachings on Jesus' Great Commandment. The *Catechism* continues,

> To catechize is "to reveal in the Person of Christ the whole of God's eternal design reaching fulfillment in that Person. It is to seek to understand the meaning of Christ's actions and words and of the signs worked by him." (426)

It is important to see basic beliefs within the context of Jesus' teaching on the kingdom of God, his life story, and the Christian story. Understanding these contexts leads to the second principle in analyzing the relationship between basic belief and story.

Stories begin with experience. The New Testament came from the faith experience of Jesus' followers as they interpreted his word and actions. Their basic beliefs came from who he was, what he taught, and their faith response to him. In other words, the New Testament is composed of interpreted faith statements, based on the community's experience and understanding of Jesus. Scripture is not abstract principles from the mouth of God, but it developed through the faith, knowledge, and wisdom of the community itself as the Spirit moved it.

Understanding the way Jesus' story received its focus through the faith of the early Christian community—especially Peter and the apostles—is critical in analyzing basic beliefs that must be interpreted in the framework of the Catholic story. This does not imply that Catholic beliefs are always well balanced. History recounts many instances of unbalanced emphases, for example, stressing the divinity of Christ while neglecting his humanity, and failing to adequately recognize God's presence in other religions. Nor does it imply that because something has not been previously taught it must be rejected in the future.

Distorting the Story

This book rests on the premise that whenever we are faithful to our stories, we experience health and vibrancy. This presumes that our stories themselves are healthy; whenever we stray too far from our stories' core elements, distortions enter.

Both health and distortions occur on a personal and communal level. Health is maintained when our stories stay in balance with who we are. For example, parents with good priorities can maintain a healthy balance between their family and their work responsibilities. Distortions can occur when parents get so immersed in their professional careers or in "bottom line" thinking that they neglect their commitment to family. Distortions occur when parents are so desirous of making money or professional advancement that they neglect their children and shift their major responsibility for the children to a babysitter or to someone else. Another kind of distortion occurs when people raised in poverty escape its clutches, succeed in business, and forget their origins. Such people make little effort to help others still engulfed in poverty, including their family members.

Once I was called to minister to an old woman living near the parish. A neighbor told me she might be starving. When I visited her I discovered that the only food she had in her home was a bottle of water: there were no canned goods or anything in the refrigerator. The woman told me that her daughter lived close by. When she gave me her name and address, I found her daughter to be living in a very affluent neighborhood. Put simply, once the daughter married a prominent businessman she neglected her poor mother, who had sacrificed to raise her.

Distortion also occurs when a group forgets the reason why it began. Some organizations and communities exhibit this trend when they stray too far from their original purpose. Take, for instance, an organization committed to raising money for the poor in Africa that sets up an elaborate organization with such high paying salaries that little money is left for the poor.

A healthy balance occurs in Church teaching and practice when the Church maintains a good balance between Jesus' story, its story, and its basic beliefs. The Church's basic beliefs must be in harmony with the Jesus' story and the Church's story.

When its leaders fail to proclaim Jesus' message of love and forgiveness, the Church strays from Jesus' story. When leaders get too involved in worldly affairs or seek political power and prestige, distortions enter Church life. Church history is filled with instances of distortion. In the Middle Ages the involvement of popes and bishops in secular affairs clouded their spiritual mission and ministry. They became powerful rulers, sometimes feared by kings and citizens alike. The popes and bishops lived more like princes than like servants.

Under the guise of protecting the Church from error, many other distortions to Jesus' story occurred. The Church was involved in brutal killings during the Crusades and in tortures during the Inquisition. Corrupt popes and bishops took mistresses and fathered children. These people neglected the truths contained in Jesus' story. They failed to see that when a person or a Christian institution strays from Jesus' core message of love, distortion results.

Both Jewish and Christian faith traditions offer a corrective that prevents its people from straying too far from God's Word. This corrective is the prophetic role. When the people strayed from God, Old Testament prophets called the Jewish nation back to belief in the one, true God. Jesus exercises his role as prophet, for example, when he upbraids the teachers who walk around in splendid robes, seek people's approval, and take first place in the synagogue, but who also take advantage of the poor (Lk 20:46–47).

After Jesus' resurrection the prophetic role shifted to the entire believing community under the leadership of the bishop of Rome and the other bishops. But this shift did not take a well-organized hierarchical form immediately after Jesus' resurrection. It took time for the early Christians to integrate the personal responsibility and freedom given to them in Christ into an institutional form.

The Holy Spirit calls the entire baptized community to a prophetic role. All Christians are to center their lives and ministry on the Great Commandment. Christians exercise a prophetic pastoral role when they teach Jesus' message accurately and completely. They exercise a prophetic critical role when they call civic and

Church leaders to account if they stray from Jesus' and the Church's story.

Distortions come from three sources. The first distortion occurs when the story is neglected. The second involves ignorance or inadequate knowledge of the basic beliefs flowing from the story. Many Catholics know little about Jesus' story and the Church's core beliefs. Such ignorance leads to errors and distortions, which range from failure to apply Church directives to business or medical issues to failing to make well-informed moral decisions. The third distortion to the story arises when the story is known, the beliefs are clear, but the interpretation takes on a self-interest that is inauthentic. The latter can result when a person or community knows Jesus' and the Church's story, as well as basic beliefs, but rationalizes one's conduct anyway. Examples of this include stealing, lying, and adultery.

A healthy Christian faith involves adherence to Jesus' story and knowledge of the Church's basic beliefs. Referring to the personal yet communal aspect of faith, the *Catechism* says,

> Faith is a personal act—the free response of the human person to the initiative of God who reveals himself. But faith is not an isolated act....The believer has received faith from others and should hand it on to others....Each believer is thus a link in the great chain of believers. (166)

Story and Basic Belief Are Complimentary

God is present in our stories. We each begin our faith journey in a particular family with two parents, at a definite moment in time, and under specific cultural conditions. In the context of our personal and family story, we interface with the Christian story. This process usually includes a relationship with our parish, with our diocese, and with the universal Church community.

Sensitivity to story and basic belief is essential for an informed Christian. Basic belief without the story is sterile, and the story without basic belief is blind. Two stories can make these points clear. When I was first ordained I gave wedding instructions to Mary and Ben, a mature couple who were both in their forties. Seminary training directed us to give four sessions to couples planning a mixed marriage, that is, a marriage where one partner is not Catholic. The first two classes went smoothly as I read from my notes, and the couple kept silent. The third session centered on sex in marriage. I nervously began. Both were married before, and the non-Catholic groom was very mature.

After reading from my seminary notes for about twenty minutes, the man stood up and signaled for his fiancée to do the same. He said, "Excuse me, Father. We're leaving now. You're a nice guy, but you don't know what you're talking about when dealing with sex in marriage. We could teach you about it, instead of you trying to teach us. We'll be back next week for the last session."

They were right. My theological lecture did not connect with their life story. I really did not know what I was talking about. It has been over forty years since that encounter, but I still remember it as if it happened yesterday. My theological lecture without the pastoral context of these people's lives was sterile. This couple taught me that I had much to learn about life in general, and that I could never pretend that I knew something when I did not.

The second story involves two students, Ellie and Fran, whom I taught in a college theology class. In one lecture I discussed the sacredness of sexuality and the need to respect our bodies. I presented the Church's basic belief that sexual activity is reserved for married life, and quoted from Pope Paul's encyclical *On Human Life*, which beautifully frames the whole issue of sexual activity within the context of Christian love.

After class, Ellie and Fran thanked me. Ellie began, "This is the first time we heard why the Church opposes premarital sexual activity. Even in Catholic schools our teachers never clearly presented the Church's teaching. In religion classes we heard over and over that God loves us and that we are to love one another. That's fine, but we needed to know more." Fran continued, "Now, we can counter some of our peers who laugh at our refusal to engage in such actions. They claim we are 'old fashioned.' Knowing the reason for the Church's teaching gives us the answers we need." Ellie and Fran's story illustrates how ignorance of why the Church opposes premarital sexuality left them blind. When they heard a good explanation, they saw clearly.

When the biblical and Church stories are not the primary references in theology and pastoral practice, distortions enter. Church Tradition helps us remain faithful to Scripture. We are encouraged to pray with Scripture, asking for the wisdom contained in the inspired texts. We look to Church Tradition, the teachings of popes, bishops, Church councils, theologians, pastors, and teachers to guide us in prayer, catechesis, and worship.

The Ministry of Theology

Catholic theologians perform their ministry within the parameters of Catholic belief and practice. Theology involves more than intellectual knowledge. It is rooted in our story, Jesus' story, and the Church's living Tradition. It centers on the Great Commandment of love. Using Jesus' story of sacrifice, compassion, and forgiveness as their starting point, theologians relate their research to the core gospel message. By connecting with the core gospel message, theologians gain a pastoral perspective. Church Fathers, who theologized in light of pastoral experience, are good models for today's theologians.

Catholic theologians need to do their research and their draw conclusions in union with the Church. Their ministry serves the Church and helps it grow. At the same time, the broader Church needs to be open to the new insights coming from theologians. The issue of the relationship between bishops and theologians often has been a sensitive one. Within proper parameters, they need to engage in meaningful dialogue with each other. Theologians need to be open to the directives of the magisterium. At the same time the magisterium can encourage the theologians to explore issues that may not be finally accepted. If done in consort, and not in the public forum of opinion, such dialogue engenders respect and can bear much fruit.

The Church has to be open to constantly expand its authentic story. If not, it will lose its energy and vigor, and some of its best ministers. Since a close connection exists between theologians, bishops, and the Catholic community, bishops and theologians are encouraged to have regular contact with each other as partners in ministry. No group has all the answers. The Church is one with many ministers, each serving different functions.

Since Jesus shares his story through his members, the laity can also offer many contributions to theology and pastoral practice. The presence of the laity insures that theology remains consistent with people's experiences. The laity energizes the Church community and brings God's Word to families and to society. Women and youth, in particular, can offer insights to help pastors and theologians deal with current needs and challenges.

Today's Church, like the early Christian community, strives for unity of faith, worship, and purpose. In so doing, it reaches out to the poor and works for justice. With trust in God and one another the Church can grow and move boldly into an uncertain future. Jesus' story gives us hope as we walk on our journey through sickness and death to resurrection and new life.

In Part One of this book, we considered the key aspects of our story, Jesus' story, and the Church's story. We now move on to Part Two, where we will take a deeper look at the connection between story and belief.

Points for Reflection
- What does Jacob's story tell you about peace and sacrifice? How would you describe the relationship between forgiveness and peace?

- How might your culture or ethnic background affect the way you respond to the Christian story, the liturgy, or to other people?

- What Christian beliefs would you say are essential? Why have you selected these beliefs?

- Reflect on the expression, "The Catholic faith begins in the Christian story."

- How do you connect your everyday activities with the basic beliefs of your faith?

- Reflect on the meaning of the expression, "The gospels are the first great Catechism."

- How do you see the connection between Jesus' story, the Church's story, your story, and basic belief?

- Why does the *Catechism of the Catholic Church* say that every believer is "a link in the great chain of believers"? What does that mean in your life? in your family life? for your work in the world?

- Many people who did not believe in Jesus admired the early Christians. Do you think Christians are admired today in the same way? Why or why not?

- To what degree do you think Jesus' story has been stressed in parish ministry, as compared to the Church's basic beliefs?

- Why is it important to take a pastoral perspective when dealing with people? How can the great saints serve as a model for today's ministers?

- What advantages are there in synthesizing basic belief?

- Reflect on the statement, "Failing to apply Jesus' story had produced dire consequences through the ages."

- To what degree was Jesus' humanity and divinity stressed in your education? Can you give examples? Was there a good balance?

- What were the most significant results of Vatican II for you? What do you see as most beneficial for the Church and for society?

- After reflecting on the history of the Church, how would you describe the relationship between story and basic belief?

- What does the Church need to do in order to continue to grow and address the needs of society?

- What is the most important insight that you gleaned from this chapter? Why does it have special significance? What does it tell you about your life?

Biblical Passages for Reflection

- Read the Acts of the Apostles. What does Acts tell you about the beginning and growth of the Church? What does it contain that is applicable to your story?

- Read the passion account of Jesus, contained in the Gospel of John (Jn 18–19). Ask God for the grace to endure difficult times, as Jesus did.

- Which gospel stories help you deal with difficult times in Church history, like the Inquisition?

- What does the story of the Good Shepherd (Jn 10:1–21) say to you? Put yourself in the place of the Good Shepherd. How can you search for those who are lost? Who is lost in your family or among your friends? What can you do to help?

Action Steps

Lessons learned. Discuss with a friend the lessons you can learn from the Church's openness to change after Vatican II. Do you see the same openness in today's Church? Do you find openness in your life?

Family discussion. Gather members of your family and discuss how your family story helps you understand the basic beliefs that you hold. Share family stories, especially stories of the older members of your household. Discuss how your faith has grown and changed.

Read the Catechism. Borrow or buy a copy of the *Catechism of the Catholic Church* and review some of the basic beliefs of the Church. Lent or Advent is a good time to do this. Set aside some time each day to accomplish this task.

Get a Church history book. Purchase a good history book about the Catholic Church or borrow one from the library or a friend. (One to consider is *Pilgrim Church* by William J. Bausch; go to www.23rdpublications.com.) If feasible, invite several friends or family members to join you and use the book as a study guide to reflect on key times in Church history.

Reach out. Seek out someone who is alienated from the Church. Be open to discuss the reasons why he or she feels alienated. If feasible, contact a compassionate Church minister or a priest to help the person begin a reconciliation process.

Learn from the past. Discuss the story of Jake and the Amish martyrs with someone. What lessons can you learn from such stories? Research the stories of Amish history on the Internet.

Visit elderly persons. Arrange to visit an elderly person and ask how the Church's basic beliefs influenced his or her life story. What are the most important aspects of his or her faith? How did such beliefs help in difficult times? If appropriate, ask if you can read a story of Jesus that has similarities to the stories told to you.

PART TWO

A Deeper Look at Story and Belief

Faith enables us to see through the eyes of Christ.

Jesus commands us to love God and one another. His message, lived out by the disciples, changed human history. As early Christians evangelized non-believers, love more than knowledge inspired people to follow the Christian path.

"See how they love one another" was the reaction of those moved by the lived reality of Jesus' message. Throughout the centuries, Christian witness to God's love has influenced the Church's effectiveness. Love, which manifests itself by how we care for our neighbor, has its foundation in faith.

Our love discloses God's love because Christianity is an incarnational religion; God's love revealed in Jesus continues through the lives of believers. ("Incarnational" in this context means that the risen Christ continues to be present in the flesh and blood witness of baptized Christians, as well as through the ministries of Word and sacrament, centered on the Eucharist.) Our love reflects God's love. We see evidence of God's love when a person is present to someone during times of both joy and pain. Few life experiences are more appreciated than a person's love and presence at key moments like birth, suffering, occasions of joy, and death.

Part One of this book described the importance of focusing on Jesus' Great Commandment in our personal story and in the Church's story. In reflecting on the history of Christianity, three virtues surfaced: faith, hope, and love. These virtues are necessary to insure the balance of story and basic belief. Part Two centers on these three theological virtues again, virtues that help us live Jesus' Great Commandment. The following chapters presume these virtues and the dynamics that underlie them. Chapter Five discusses story and faith, and considers story and basic belief through the lens of Christian faith. Chapter Six considers story, basic beliefs, and practices through the lens of Christian love. Chapter Seven reflects on story, basic belief, and identity through the lens of Christian hope.

Chapter Five

Looking through the Lens of Christian Faith

"Now I have told you this before it occurs,
so that when it does occur, you may believe." (Jn 14:29)

Our response to the Christian story and its basic beliefs rests on faith. In Matthew we see this faith in action as John the Baptist preaches a baptism of water for the repentance of sin. Accepting this baptism required faith, as did accepting John's words that Jesus would baptize with the Holy Spirit and fire (Mt 3:11–12). Jesus is the light of the world, a light that the darkness cannot overcome (Jn 1:1–5). All the gospels begin with Jesus bringing new light into the world. To recognize the new vision that Jesus' light offers, faith is necessary.

The gospels reflect the disciples' weak faith during Jesus' lifetime and the ambiguity of their faith following Jesus' resurrection. While Mary Magdalene, Peter, and the other disciples sensed that something unusual happened at the resurrection, their uncertainty and doubt filled the air. The lack of faith at the resurrection is symbolized by Thomas' refusal to believe and by the inability of the two apostles on the road to Emmaus to recognize the stranger as Jesus. Were the disciples afraid? They staked their whole future on Jesus; perhaps they were hesitant to believe again.

Luke says that Mary of Magdala, Joanna, and Mary, Jesus' mother, told the apostles and disciples what they had seen and heard at the tomb. The two men with dazzling garments reminded them of Jesus' words—that he had to die and would rise again on the third day. Luke says, "these words seemed to them an idle tale, and they did not believe them" (Lk 24:11).

On the evening of that same day two disciples left Jerusalem and headed toward Emmaus. Were they running away? Were they unwilling to risk starting over with Jesus? Scripture does not say, but it indicates that as the two proceeded on their journey, "Jesus himself came near and went with them, but their eyes were kept from recognizing him" (Lk 24:15–16). After he asked them what they were debating, they told him all that had happened to Jesus during the previous days. He responded, "Oh, how foolish you are, and how slow of heart to believe all that the prophets have declared"(Lk 24:25).

Jesus explained the Scripture passages that referred to him, but they still did not understand that the stranger before them was Jesus. When they reached their destination, Jesus acted as if he was going on. They urged him to stay and they entered a home to eat the evening meal. As they ate, Jesus blessed bread and offered it to them. At that moment, their eyes were opened and they knew the stranger before them was Jesus.

The two disciples failed to recognize Jesus on the road. Did they lack faith? Their frustration, anger, and disappointment had shattered their weak faith following the crucifixion. After his resurrection, even though Jesus was present, they did not recognize him.

The Relationship Between Story and Faith

This gospel story invites us to reflect on the relationship between story and faith. By our reflection, we learn that faith enables us to see differently. Faith enables us to see through the eyes of Christ. We experience the same joys and troubles. We live the same life at home and work. We have the same opportunities and temptations.

With faith, however, we deal with them differently. We see them in light of Jesus' Great Commandment of love. Money and position are not as important as love, justice, and compassion. Because we have faith, we take more time with our families and see a poor person as a neighbor made in the image of Christ.

We often fail to see life through the eyes of faith. Even though we sincerely try to imitate Christ, sometimes we do not recognize God's presence in our everyday lives. We do not recognize Jesus as the light of the world in the menial events of our day.

When reflecting on the story of the two apostles on the road to Emmaus, I recall my situation before I had a cataract operation. Before surgery, my vision was dull and I did not fully recognize that it was dull. The dullness occurred over such a long time that I did not appreciate what was going on. I saw little, and what I saw was blurred. My vision was gradually shutting off. Our vision is dulled when we fail to see life through Jesus' eyes and see it through worldly eyes.

After my operation, my eyes cleared, and everything around me was light and vibrant. My new vision did not happen overnight; it took time. When we try to change from worldly ways to God's ways it takes time. Temptation and failure often beset us, but if we keep trying God's grace will conquer. Sin and lack of faith blind us. We are destined to live forever, but without faith the meaning of our lives remains unclear. With faith, we see life in a new way. Like human vision, spiritual vision depends on the lens through which we look. If we look through secular eyes, sickness and death have no meaning. Through the eyes of faith, however, such powerful experiences are stages on our journey with God. They link us with a transcendent realm whose origin and goal is our Creator.

An awareness of God's presence is a vital component of our relationship with God and neighbor. Through faith's eyes, words and actions reflect the God who lives and pulsates in our story, Jesus' story, and the Church's story. Faith clarifies how God is with us and opens new horizons in our life quest.

What is the relationship between faith, story, and basic belief? We must consider story and personal presence and the relationship between community, story, and belief (both the within and the without of the story). We must decide the beginning point: is it story or belief? Finally, we must unpack the story.

Personal Presence

When I think of my mother, I think of her life—not her death. I remember her faith and love and how she was always there for our family and friends, especially when I was a child. I remember, in particular, when I became very sick several weeks just after beginning the first grade. The doctor told my parents that I needed complete rest for about eight months and that if I did not rest, I might not live. The doctor told them, "Bob has looked forward to attending school, but this is not possible. He will have to repeat the first grade."

When my mother heard the doctor's decision, she asked him, "If I go to his school and get the lessons from his teacher, I can teach him at home. Is this okay?" The doctor gave his permission as long as the first grade teacher concurred. Every day my mother left the house, walked to St. William's School, and returned home with the lessons for the next day. Faithfully she taught me what the other students learned. She constantly gave me hope and reminded me that I would get well. Near the school year's end, when I returned to school, I was two weeks ahead of the class.

During that year the most important lessons I learned were not from the excellent instructions that my mother gave me. The most important lessons came from her faith in God and her presence with me six hours a day for eight months. Later I realized that my mother was committed to me because God was present with her. From her I learned God's love and presence in my life in ways that went beyond what she taught me from schoolbooks. Through her example God became part of my life. My mother's love and God's presence with me has grown stronger over the years. From her faith and dedication, I first learned how God's love lives in our love for one another, and when we are present to each other in faith.

I recall a conversation my mother and I had one day, many years later. "Mom, you spend almost every moment of every day by yourself in this house. Do you ever get lonely here?" She replied, "Never! I do chores each day, like sewing, cleaning, or cooking something special for you. I pray and reflect on Scripture every morning, read in the afternoon, and never watch television until late in the day. If I watch it too much, my mind will get rusty."

As Mom answered me, she glanced down the hall from her chair. I said, "Do you feel God's presence with you?" She replied, "Yes, Bob. Not long ago, I saw Jesus at the end of the hall by Mary's picture. I didn't tell anyone else, but I tell you. I know you will understand and not think I am silly."

That afternoon Mom and I sat in the backyard, near the grassy area that I enclosed for her and her dog. The yard faced the farm next door. Beyond the fields, massive trees stood at the edge of a hill that led down to the Ohio River. Majestic clouds swirled above and partially enveloped the trees. In a reflective moment I asked, "Mom, you often sit for hours with your dog. Do you experience God in this place?" She replied, "Yes, Bob. It's easy to pray here. It is so quiet, except for an occasional bird or deer. Everything is beautiful. I get a strong feeling of God's presence with me. As I look into the clouds, I sometimes see an image that reminds me of God."

As Mom approached her ninetieth birthday, she spent most of her time at home. When I was with her, she usually sat in her reclining chair as I sat on a sofa nearby. Often when I celebrated Mass, I sensed her presence next to me.

I knew that after her death I would want to remember such moments. How true this is. Every evening after night prayers, I think of Mom in her chair near me. This inevitably triggers a sense of her presence with me and her love for me. The Risen Christ and the spirits of the dead now with God transcend the bonds of space and time. Those who have died can communicate spiritually with us. How reasonable it is that those who deeply loved us on earth continue to manifest themselves to us.

Scripture narrates that Jesus was the same but different after the resurrection. Why should we expect it to be different with those who have achieved their eternal reward and are now with Jesus in his risen, glorified body? While we wait to see them again, our faith gives the consolation that they are still near.

God's love, revealed in Jesus, took concrete shape in his teaching and actions. Who he was rather than what he said deeply affected his friends, neighbors, and enemies. The power of his presence is seen in the way Jesus dealt with Lazarus (Jn 11:1–44), the Samaritan woman at the well (Jn 4:1–42), the paralytic (Lk 5:17–26), and the leper who returned to give thanks (Lk 17:11–19). The stories of Jesus' passion and crucifixion also describe a man who was present to those around him.

Although Jesus was present to those around him, he also spent considerable time in solitude. Christians have mirrored Jesus' balance of contemplation and action. We find a balance of quiet and action when we get away from our busyness and invite God to come to us when we are alone. Sometimes we may not feel God's presence. In spite of God's apparent absence during these times we take heart from Jesus' promise that he will remain with us always. When lonely or alone we need to pray with the confidence that God hears us. By praying, trust in God becomes an integral part of life.

The Within and Without of the Story

The story of Jesus' death and resurrection can be seen through the "faith lens" of Christians who experience sickness and death. Life experiences like pain and sorrow provide occasions to connect with faith. We begin from within by relating our emotions, thoughts, and feelings to our beliefs. Because the focus of our experience is the "within" of our lives, we call this the "within" of the story.

Jesus' death and resurrection fulfills Scripture. His death and resurrection occurred outside of our personal experience, but they are intimately related to us because they brought our salvation. When our starting point for reflection begins outside of our lives (in the Old Testament, Jesus' teaching, or the Church's tradition and beliefs), we call this the "without" of the story. Both the within and the without of the story are necessary. The approach taken depends on the circumstances, experiences, people, and reasons for the reflections. They are two sides of the same coin.

The Beginning Point: Story or Belief?

In analyzing story and belief, we sometimes begin with the story itself. We live, tell, or hear a story and then draw our conclusions or beliefs from the story. Or we can start with our beliefs, draw insights from them, then apply them to our story. In either case, we need to ask the Holy Spirit to lead and guide us.

The relationship between story and belief is not an "either/or," but a "both/and." The most complete analysis of story and belief comes from the intersection of the within and without of the story in the context of community. We can see the importance of the story's within and without by analyzing the Emmaus story. Initially the disciples began with the within of Jesus' death and resurrection; they recount their experiences and those of the disciples. They drew no clear conclusions in recounting what happened to Jesus. When Jesus came along, their lack of faith prevented them from recognizing him. His explanation of Old Testament prophecies and his breaking bread (the without) opened their eyes.

Reflecting on the Emmaus story helps us see that good theological and pastoral analysis requires theology from within (beginning with story) and theology from without (beginning with basic belief). In every instance our analysis must take into account the believing community.

Unpacking the Story

Every story starts with God. Our story begins as our parents cooperate with God's creative activity in conceiving us. The early experiences we have impact on our subsequent values. Some personal, pastoral, or theological reflections begin with a story that addresses meaning and belief. I addressed meaning and belief when I began this book with the story of my mother's death. Other reflections begin by having recourse to beliefs, teachings, research, or authoritative statements. An example of this would be when a teacher quotes a passage and discusses it.

When unpacking the story and learning from it, we must know our personal gifts and the audience that we address. Sometimes it is more beneficial to begin with beliefs or teachings, at other times it is better to begin with story.

When reflecting on my mother's death in Chapter One, I considered the within of the story. As I held her hand I thought of Mary holding Jesus' dead body. I saw my mother's life and death in light of basic Catholic beliefs. I unpacked this aspect of my mother's story beginning from the within of her life on earth. After thinking about her love, I reflected on her life in light of Jesus' and the Church's story and Catholic beliefs. When I felt emotionally strong enough to tell the story of her death, I described how I held her hand after she died. I drew out the pastoral implications of holding her hand in light of Jesus' death and resurrection. Telling this story often touches deep aspects of other people's stories, who relive the death of a loved one through my story about my mother. Touching a deep level of life indicates the story's power.

Jesus taught through stories because he knew they touched his hearers' minds and hearts. On some occasions he drew lessons from his stories to clarify his intention in telling them. At other times the lessons were so apparent that they needed no further explanation. At still other times the community understood the story's meaning only later on. When we tell stories in class, lectures, and homilies, we may need to help people draw meaning from them. Short segment thinking does not encourage us to see bigger pictures or draw adequate conclusions. We often need help in discerning a story's implications and applications.

Some people prefer to begin with the story and then connect it with basic belief. Others would rather start with basic belief. The Catholic Church today strives to strengthen the content materials in the catechesis of children, youth, and adults. To accomplish this goal many catechists, teachers, and bishops concentrate on teaching basic Catholic beliefs. They use the beliefs, rather than the stories, to teach. This certainly is acceptable, but if we begin with belief, it is important to connect these beliefs with the deep dimension of story. If this connection does not occur, beliefs remain abstract and learners often do not appreciate them.

No real separation exists between story and basic belief. As we unpack a story to discover the deep values and beliefs that it manifests, we need to maintain a balance between story and its community component. This is the backdrop for looking at stories, basic beliefs, and practices through the lens of Christian love. We consider these dimensions in Chapter Six.

Points for Reflection

- Discuss the relationship between faith and your awareness of God. What personal stories came to mind after you reflected on the lack of faith of the early followers of Christ? What can you learn from such reflections?

- How does faith in a person or God help us see differently?

- What story from your life helps you appreciate the close relationship between the presence of another person and the development of your faith? Have you experienced care similar to that described by the author when he was in the first grade? How did the experience affect you?

- When do you feel the presence of God most intimately in your life? What, if anything, did this experience of God have to do with the presence or absence of a loved one?

- What does God's presence mean to you when you are lonely and hurting?

- Discuss the need not only to know Jesus' story but also to convey his teaching accurately and completely. How well do you think the Church has done this during the past twenty-five years?

- What significance do you see in the distinction between theology from within and theology from without? What is your starting point—within or without—and why?

- What is the most important insight that you gleaned from this chapter? Why does it have special significance? What does it tell you about your life?

Biblical Passages for Reflection

- Read the resurrection accounts in the four gospels (Mt 28, Mk 16, Lk 24, Jn 20). Compare similarities and differences in each account. Reflect on the disciples' fear and uncertainty and consider experiences in your life when you felt similar experiences. Meditate also on the faint glimmer of hope that must have sustained Jesus' followers. Reflect on the need for hope in your life when things are not going well.

- What do you feel Mary experienced just after the resurrection?

- Reflect on the story of the two apostles on the road to Emmaus (Lk 24:13–35). Discuss what this story tells you about the need to develop the virtue of hope. How do you compare the need for faith in these stories to your need for faith in difficult times?

Action Steps

Lessons learned. Discuss with a friend the lessons you can learn from looking more seriously at the relationship between your story and your basic beliefs. How consistent have they been in your life? If you find any inconsistency between your beliefs and the teachings of the Church, take the time to look more deeply at the reasons for the Church's teachings. Begin with prayer, asking the Holy Spirit for guidance.

Family discussion. Gather members of your family and discuss important aspects of your family's story. At the same time, consider how well family members know Jesus' story and the basic teachings of their faith. Share stories and indicate how your faith has grown and changed. Ask each person to do the same.

Lent or Advent learning. Attend a faith formation series in your parish to help you deepen and better appreciate your faith. Buy a recent compendium of Catholic beliefs and practices, read it, and share what you learned with family members or friends. Encourage your parish leaders to develop spiritual sessions, centering on Scripture and basic beliefs during these seasons.

Buy a Bible. If you do not have a family Bible, buy one. Invite the family to read passages from it every evening after dinner or at another time, such as a family lenten devotion.

Reach out. Seek out someone who has been hurt in some way by the Church. Pray about the situation, asking guidance from the Holy Spirit. If appropriate, offer to discuss what happened. If the person is open, invite the individual to attend liturgy with you and introduce the person to an understanding pastoral minister.

Learn from your loved ones. Remember painful times when you or a family member was sick, lost a job, or suffered a serious setback. Keep a journal of your feelings and conclusions about what you learned from such experiences.

Visit a needy person. Visit suffering family members, friends, or others in a retirement home. Pray with them and share what you learned during difficult times in your life. Listen and thank them for sharing their lives with you. If appropriate, ask if you can read a story of Jesus that sheds some insight into what you have discussed.

Chapter Six

Looking through the Lens of Christian Love

See then, beloved, what a great and wonderful thing love is,
and how inexpressible its perfection…. (Liturgy of the Hours,
Tuesday of the Second Week of Ordinary Time)

The theological virtue of love underpins the human story and the Judeo-Christian faith tradition. This chapter looks at story and core beliefs through the lens of the Great Commandment. It considers living the cross, the role of community as it connects to the core meaning of Christian love, and the power of the story as it touches our human core.

Living the Cross

The old, tarnished chalice rests in a black box. It has not been used for many years. The style reflects the consecrated cups once used by priests of a bygone era. Its Latin inscription recalls a time when the Latin Mass was a powerful focal point of Catholic life and worship. Underneath the chalice is the name of the priest who once used it. His name was Leonard. The inscription says his parents gave the chalice to him at his priestly ordination. Many such chalices exist in dark corners of old churches and priest houses. Their original owners' stories are lost in the annals of history. This chalice, however, is different. Its owner is known and so is some of its history.

Without the history behind it, the chalice would be only a sacred vessel. With the history, it is much more. It symbolizes a beautiful but painful life, centered in love of God and neighbor. We know the history in its rudimentary outlines because the chalice belonged to a family who preserves it with pride. The facts surrounding it have been passed down through the priest's family. Here is how the family remembers it.

Shortly before the outbreak of World War II, Leonard was ordained. For months his family exuded enthusiasm, as they anticipated his visit home before he would proceed to the Orient for his first assignment. They anxiously waited the day of his arrival by preparing banners and cards.

On a beautiful summer afternoon, Leonard finally returned home. He was a handsome, intelligent, athletic man, full of energy and hope. He told his parents, brother, sister, cousins, and all present that he could not wait to bring the Word of God's love to the Orient. That day he spoke words in a strange language. The adults' only response was to smile and wonder what they meant. The children thought these words sounded funny. Soon this wonderful day was over and the family wished Leonard well. In the evening he left to catch a train to California. From there a boat took him to the Orient. Leonard took his chalice with him.

In the ensuing months, the family received many letters from him as he traveled to his assignment. Finally, one letter said that he arrived. In time his letters became fewer in number, and those that the family received implied that things were not going well. They described the bombing by enemy aircraft. Fear and anxiety replaced his joyful messages. Then family heard no more.

Almost a year passed. The family thought that he had been killed; he was listed as missing. One day a priest from his order called Leonard's sister and told her that Leonard was in a hospital a thousand miles from his mission camp. Leonard had had a severe mental breakdown and was flown to the hospital in a small plane. Most of what happened to him remains unknown.

Eventually Leonard returned to the United States and was detained in a mental hospital. In the years before depressants and other drugs to treat mental illness, the condition of such institutions was often deplorable. Patients yelled and howled as a visitor walked through the wards. Many were tied down.

When Leonard's brother saw how and where he was housed, he cried. He was overcome with grief because he scarcely recognized Leonard when he walked toward him. His brother brought Leonard home. Family members could not believe what had happened to him. He was different than the vibrant, young man that left for the Orient two years previous. Leonard was a broken man, with mood swings and other physical and mental symptoms. He stayed in his parents' home and with his siblings. Were it not for them and the kindness of the local parish priest, the family still wonders what would have happened to him.

Leonard remained at home for several years. Gradually he began saying Mass, settled down, and improved somewhat even though he was unable to function in a fully normal way. It was clear that Leonard would not be able to resume normal duties as a priest. By the time he returned to his provincial headquarters, Leonard had lived an unbelievable life—and this before he was thirty years old. He stayed in various community houses throughout the years and came home every once in a while. Although he celebrated Mass daily, he preached only a few times during the rest of his life.

Over the years, Leonard tried to go to the missions, but he was unable to function. As he grew older, he painted, played cards, and worked in the library. After his parents died, he rarely returned home. Eventually a doctor found a drug to help his mental condition. Leonard became reflective and mystical as he aged. The last time a family member visited him, she found him alone in chapel. Leonard told her, "I spend much of the day in chapel. I pray and say the rosary. I already said five of them before you came."

Leonard spent his last twenty-five years at his order's provincial headquarters. When Leonard died in his mid-seventies, his Mass of Christian Burial was celebrated in the community chapel. Family members expected only a few priests, sisters, and laity to attend, and they were surprised to see the many people who attended. The family wondered, "Why did people come that no one seemed to know? Who were they?" Apparently, some townspeople knew Leonard. He talked to them on his afternoon walks. They admired him and paid him tribute the day he was buried. Sisters in a community near his residence also came. Often he gave them simple gifts. His family members then understood why Leonard often told them that he spent some of his monthly allowance to buy gifts for those he visited.

In reflecting on Leonard's life, it is easy to appreciate why Jesus taught that love helps heal our broken human condition. Jesus sent the Holy Spirit so that he might live through his broken members. Leonard did not spend his life preaching sermons from the pulpit or catechizing children. His preaching was more difficult. He accomplished it through faithful testimony and the love of God and neighbor. His suffering enabled him to reach beyond the limits of human endurance because he believed in the love of the Risen Christ. His life became a living sermon. Jesus asks all Christians to preach this sermon through their love of God and neighbor.

When we stand before God and account for our lives, may we be as fortunate as Leonard. Leonard's faith allowed him to live out his vocation in his limited situation. He did it on God's terms, not his own, because he recognized God's love for him. As he took up his cross, the words of the first letter of John are appropriate: "Those who abide in love abide in God, and God abides in them" (1 Jn 4:16b).

Many years after Leonard's return from the Orient, his family received a telephone call from a pawn shop operator. Someone had pawned a chalice with Leonard's name inscribed on it. After his family identified it as Leonard's, the ordination chalice was returned to him. How it made its way to the pawnshop no one knows. Its history is mysterious, similar to the designs that God had for Leonard. Broken mentally and physically in the war, Leonard never became bitter or abandoned his faith or vocation. His love of God and neighbor drew him close to God.

After Leonard's death, his sister asked for his chalice, which she gave to her son. He keeps it as a symbol of Leonard's courage and love. It is a living reminder of what it signifies, namely, the suffering, death, and resurrection of Jesus who lives through the joys and sufferings of his body, the Church. It symbolizes men and women who, like Leonard, are faith-filled enough to take up their crosses and follow Jesus in love.

What actually happened to Leonard in the Orient will never be fully known. It does not matter. What does matter, however, is that his life story (and every person's story) discloses the image of Christ. After his sickness, the quality of Leonard's life changed, but the quality of Christ's life in him remained and intensified until the day he received his eternal reward in heaven.

By unpacking stories like Leonard's, we can appreciate a story's value in helping us unravel life's mysteries. Leonard's story indicates that all human love comes from God, who is love. This is reflected beautifully in an ancient letter of Pope Clement I to the Corinthians, who speaks of committed Christians says:

> Let the (one) truly possessed by the love of Christ keep his commandments. Who can express the binding power of divine love? Who can find words for the splendor of its beauty? Beyond all description are the heights to which it lifts us. Love unites us to God; it cancels innumerable sins, has no limits to its endurance, bears everything patiently. Love is neither servile nor arrogant....By it all God's chosen ones have been sanctified; without it, it is impossible to please....The Lord Jesus Christ gave his life's blood for us— he gave his body for our body, his soul for our soul.

Community of Love

The community's role is vital in appreciating any story. The Christian community contains the dynamic of love that makes appreciation possible. The Christian story begins in the communal love of the Three Persons of the Trinity. Out of love God created the earth. God's divine initiative reached fullness in the creation of humans, who are made in God's image. The Christian community builds upon the foundation of love first disclosed to the Jews. God's initial revelation, coming through them, continues in the Church.

We discover God's love through creation, especially through the faith and good example of parents and family. As I reflected on several volumes of old letters from family members I have on my bookshelf, I realized that God's love is revealed through family. The letters describe our family's home life when I was a student in the seminary. People cannot understand the love in these letters unless they know our family's faith.

Our family set the stage for the way that we related to each other and others. My relationship with my father illustrates this point. When I was a boy my father taught me how to use a hammer, play baseball, and work in our dry goods store. He heard my homework, took me to Mass, prayed with me, and arranged our annual vacation trip. During such times, a bond developed between us that went beyond what we did or said. Even in times of sickness, his love of God, family, and neighbor strengthened us.

My father died over twenty years ago. I spent his last day on earth with him. We sat alone in his hospital room. When I touched his hand, he looked at me with peaceful eyes. As our glances met, I knew this would be our last time together. We smiled and I said, "Dad, thanks for everything. I love you." His smile broadened and peace came over him. We prayed and I gave him my final blessing. As I left I kissed him on the forehead. He closed his eyes when I said "Good-bye, Dad. I love you." He answered, "Good-bye, Bob. I love you too," shifted slightly, and slept.

Since my father's death, I often hear him speaking to me in the context of God's love. It is as if his voice and God's voice merged. This communication goes beyond his words that I hear in my mind. I feel warmth, love, peace, and joy in my whole body, as if God's love wraps my father and I together.

One occasion stands out. I visited his grave eight months after he died. A large oak tree a short distance from his burial spot provided a wonderful backdrop for a large crucifix that rested twenty feet away. The sunlight sparkled through the trees and changed the darkness of the cross into the brightness of a new day. As I stood at the foot of his grave, a warm, loving feeling came over me. I felt the deepest peace that I can remember. My father was with me. His body lay at my feet but his spirit filled my heart. He, God, and I were joined together. I heard his voice. It was almost as if his voice and God's voices were indistinguishable. God spoke words of peace through him. I heard, "Bob, I am with God. There is no reason to fear, for God's love is greater than fear. Have faith, let go, and be with me and your God."

As I listened, the sunlight struck the small flowers on his grave, telling me that light overcomes darkness and fear. I did not want to leave that place but soon knew it was time to go. As I walked toward my car, the day's radiance filled me, as the sun struck my shoulders and illuminated my vision. I recalled the words of the Song of Solomon, "Love is strong as death….Its flashes are flashes of fire, a raging flame." (Song 8:6). On that day I experienced a love that no flood can quench and no torrent can drown.

Although God's love often is manifested through people, God's love goes beyond such experiences. At my father's gravesite God was present in a profound way. We sometimes feel a deep presence of God when walking alone in the woods, meditating in a church, or praying in our room. Jesus had similar experiences of God when he went alone to the mountain to pray and when he agonized in the garden before his crucifixion. During my father's last days, I wondered what he thought about and how he felt when he was alone. In reality he never was alone; God was with him.

Any story must be interpreted in light of the community that framed it. In the Emmaus story, Jesus' disciples interpreted what happened from Good Friday to Easter Sunday. Their interpretations were affected by the broader community story, including the story of the Jewish people and Jesus' last days. Initially the two disciples on the road to Emmaus failed to understand. Without the bigger story, which Jesus provided, they could not grasp that Jesus was the Messiah.

Community is the backdrop in which any story originates; community offers rich insights into the story's meaning. Basic beliefs emerge from the story's foundation in community, which in the Christian community is the Great Commandment. Jesus promised to send the Holy Spirit to insure his message of love would be preached and to keep the Church free from serious error when interpreting the meaning of Jesus' story. The Spirit continues to inspire us to love and to preserve the Church from error in interpreting core aspects of Jesus' story. The Spirit also inspires us to cooperate with God's graces to make the theological virtue of love the hub around which we frame our words, deeds, and very lives.

Love Connects at the Core

Why do the stories of my parents' death touch me so deeply? Why do they differ in intensity from mere descriptions of what happened? The answer comes down to the difference between a story and an example. Any meaningful story touches the core of human life and connects the hearer with a reality that goes beyond all of us. This realm is at the heart of human life. The heart of a story connects with the mysteries of why we were born, why we suffer, why we die, and what happens after death. Core stories bring us into contact with God, the source and goal of life. By entering into the story, we enter the realm of the holy.

A story that touches our life's core is rooted in love. It establishes a foundation for human identity, which implies sharing in God's nature of holy love. In Scripture, this love is first manifested in the

Genesis stories of creation. God created humans in God's own image and likeness (Gn 1:26–31). Whenever a story connects with love, the font of life itself, it evokes a deep response. All the core questions of living and dying are framed around the need to love and be loved according to God's commandments. In one way or another, every core question connects with the mystery of God's love and the human need to respond to God's love as a creature who was born to love. Without love we lose our connection with our deepest core and with those we are commanded to love. In the stories about my mother and father this need to love and be loved is clear. Their stories touch ultimate dimensions of life and connect with God, the source of life.

On the other hand, an example never reaches such depths. An example cannot touch the realm of the holy, satisfy the longings of the human heart, or answer ultimate questions. Examples are functional. They describe ways to get along in this world; they are the means to an end, not the end itself. The computer I use to write this book helps me write my thoughts and feelings, which may inspire the reader to a greater sense of meaning and purpose. The book is a means, whereas the stories told in this book are intended to touch a deeper meaning in life. Stories ground basic Christian beliefs and beliefs clarify the meaning of stories.

Love always happens in relationship, and love begins in the relationships in the Trinity. From the relationships of the Father, the Son, and the Holy Spirit, divine love is poured out upon the world. Because of this divine love, Jesus redeemed us after we had sinned. Because of God's love dwelling within us, we can love. Because God enters into relationship with us, we are commanded to love our neighbor as ourselves. By our love we continue the love pact initiated between God and humankind. Stories that reflect such love touch us and move us to thank God for our lives and inspire us to reach out to the needy.

When my father and mother died, their love set the foundation for their greatest act of love: they offered their final suffering to

God as Jesus did, with faith that God would raise them up as God raised Jesus from the dead.

Why do we see our life story through the lens of love? Why does it have meaning in the face of failure and death? Our core Christian beliefs tell us that, like Jesus, our suffering and death will be transformed into the glory because we have believed and loved.

The Power of All Stories

Love is the key connection between human life and the story, yet stories of violence, hatred, and lust have such an attractive force. Why? These negative stories also touch deep dimensions of human existence, though far differently than stories filled with love. The attractive force of evil is evident in the story of Adam and Eve, the second creation account of Genesis (2:5—3:24). The Jews included this second creation story in the Scriptures as a counterpoint to the first creation account (1:1—2:4), which stresses the world's basic goodness. The first creation story describes the world as God intended it to be; the second shows what happens when humans disregard God's designs: misery and death. Though different than the power of love and goodness, sin's attractive power also touches life's core.

Evil is attractive because it is a counter symbol of God's designs. We are free to say "yes" or "no" to God. When we say "no" to God, we make ourselves into gods and fly in the face of the one, true God. Even when we turn way from God, however, God continues to love us. God even sent his Son to redeem us from our sins.

The Christian story and basic beliefs reflect God's love, manifested in Scripture, in the Church, and in faithful people. The Christian story discloses the depths of God's love. Community and basic beliefs emerge from the story of God's love. The theological virtue of love gives us a sense of who we are in light of our story and beliefs. Chapter Seven reflects on story and belief as they frame Christian identity in the context of the theological virtue of hope.

Points for Reflection

- What does Leonard's story tell you about success in life?

- Is there a mentally challenged person in your family or among your friends or neighbors? What is your attitude toward him or her? What have you learned from this person? Could you say he or she is gifted by God? Why or why not?

- Why is community important in both story and belief?

- Reflect on a person in your family who was particularly present to you in a difficult time. How did that person's faith influence his or her attitude toward you? How was faith conveyed? What does this tell you about your need to be present to other family members, friends, colleagues, and work associates?

- Reflect on one story in your life that is particularly connected to the core dimension of your life. How did this event impact your faith and basic belief?

- Reflect on times that the virtue of love motivated you and kept you going in the midst of difficulties. Share your reflections with a trusted friend or family member.

- Which stories from your life do the stories in this chapter bring to mind?

- What is the most important insight that you gleaned from this chapter? Why does it have special significance? What does it tell you about your life?

Biblical Passages for Reflection

- Reflect on the Beatitudes (Mt 5:1–12) in light of Jesus' special blessing of mentally, emotionally, and physically challenged persons. Jesus tells us we are the "salt of the earth" and the "light of the world" (Mt 5:13, 14). How do these words apply to Leonard? How do they apply to you? How are they especially applicable when you are sick, broken, and vulnerable?

- Find a biblical passage that indicates that story and basic belief reflect God's love. Share your reflections in a group, with another person, or write them down in a notebook or journal and pray with them.

Action Steps

Visit the mentally challenged. Learn about homes for mentally challenged people in your area and visit someone who does not have regular visitors.

Find family stories. From old family letters or personal reflections gather important stories that tell your family's past. Invite family members to come together to tell significant stories and reflect on them. What do these stories, letters, or reflections say to you as a family and as an individual? What are the connections between these stories and their faith? What can you learn from them about your faith and your family's faith today?

Visit a cemetery. The bodies of the dead are sacred. Those close to us deserve honor and prayer. In reflection on your family or personal story, remember persons of particular significance, visit their graves, and pray for them.

Offer a Mass. Remember the people who have influenced your faith who have died. During Advent or Lent or on their birthday, have a Mass offered in your parish for their intentions.

Tell a story. Gather younger family members and tell them the story of their ancestors. Tell the story during in a celebration at home, such as a potluck dinner with relatives or a picnic. The celebrative style coupled with stories and prayers gives the younger generation an indication of the family's gratitude for those who have gone before. Tell the young people that their stories, too, will be part of the family's tradition one day.

Chapter Seven

Looking through the Lens of Christian Hope

*We have heard of your faith in Christ Jesus and of the love you have
for all the saints, because of the hope laid up for you in heaven....
Provided that you continue securely established and
steadfast in the faith, without shifting from the hope
promised by the gospel. (Col 1:4–5, 23)*

These words of Colossians offer a message of hope and indicate the
importance of this Christian virtue. I learned its significance in
childhood through the example of my parents, family, and Church.

Made in God's Image

One day when a man in a restaurant said, "Hi, Bob!" I responded,
"Hi, Jim. It's been a long while since we've seen one another." Jim
and I discussed growing up in the same neighborhood and our
time as classmates in grade school and high school. As we reflected
on our Catholic upbringing, I thought about the early years of my
faith, a time in which I was inspired with hope.

Christian hope is a gift of God that my parents nourished within
me through their example, prayers, and teaching even before I
began school. They taught me that life is beautiful and worthwhile.

They reminded me that I have a role in life and that I should look forward to it, whatever it is. In short, they instilled hope in me, and hope is a vital part of who I am.

My childhood set the foundation for the gradual clarification of my beliefs at home and in school. In the second grade I received a religion book with a gray paper cover. I wondered what it was since I did not understand its title: *A Catechism of Christian Doctrine*, #1. My teacher said it contained the basic Catholic beliefs in question and answer form. In lesson five, the *Catechism* described who I am (my identity). It says that human beings are creatures "composed of body and soul and made to the image and likeness of God." After my teacher explained what it means to be created in God's image, I saw more clearly who I was called to be by God. I thought, "If I am made in God's image, I am supposed to live as God wants me to live." This made me feel special, and I grew in hopeful anticipation of God's blessings.

As a child, I connected being made in God's image with another question, namely, "Why did God make us?" The *Catechism* said, "God made us to show forth his goodness and to share with us his everlasting happiness in heaven." The *Catechism* taught me that I could look forward in hope to life on earth and eternal life in heaven. I learned that God will bless me if I live a good life. I realized that my life's purpose was connected with getting to heaven. Happiness on earth and the hope of eternal happiness in heaven became my great motivators.

These two catechism answers frame my entire life. The first tells me who I am; the second indicates my destiny. The first gives me identity; the second offers me hope. My analysis of identity and hope are more sophisticated now, but my identity is rooted in my story and the basic beliefs that I learned from my parents, teachers, and the *Catechism*. My early faith education taught me that God lives within me. I am a person who is to live a good life, and I am hopeful that God will reward me for doing so. God's goodness and love make me who I am: God's child.

This chapter reflects on story, belief, and identity through the lens of Christian hope. What are identity, story, and belief? Within a story context, what kinds of identities are there? What connections are there between hope, story, and life?

Identity, Story, and Belief

My identity refers to who I am. When I consider my identity superficially, I regard myself as an American male. If I go deeper, I see my role in my family and I see myself as a priest of a certain age and ethnic background. As I probe the issue even further, I look at who I am at the core of my being. There I am a person created in God's image, and my destiny to live forever.

My childhood experiences, including a sense of belonging, affected my identity. In probing my identity, I look at my life's story and consider my family background, faith, aspirations, and hopes; each touches the core of who I am.

Identity is deeper than the roles we play in society. Identity has a spiritual level, and this spiritual level is the root of our search for meaning. On the spiritual level, core issues of God, personal responsibilities, birth, life, and the afterlife help us discern who we are. If we fail to consider these core issues, our search for identity remains shallow.

Our core identity remains the same throughout life, although it shifts focus according to our age and circumstances as we assume new tasks and let go of old ones. Identity indicates our life's connections with others, and hope keeps us focused on our final goal.

Early in life I learned that to fulfill my life's goal, I must live as Jesus commanded me to live in the Great Commandment. By living the Great Commandment I discover my true identity. If I fail to live as Jesus directs me to live, I fail to discover my true identity as a child of God.

Christian identity is intimately connected with baptism. Through baptism we enter a new relationship with the Trinity that gives us the hope promised by Jesus to those who love him. My par-

ents offered me this living hope when they assumed their responsibilities as Christian parents at my baptism. They lived out the
mystery of Jesus' dying and rising by sacrificing themselves for our
family. During my sickness and during the death of my father and
mother, hope gave me confidence that God was with me, no matter what might happen.

Kinds of Identity in a Story Context

We learn to understand who we are as we relate to God, the world,
and other people. Coming to appreciate our identity happens differently for each person. There are relational, personal, and contextual identities that can be seen through the lens of hope.

Relational Identity and Hope

Relational identity is identity as part of a community, family, or
group. Jews center their lives on Yahweh's covenant promise to
them. God's saving message was given to the entire people. Jesus
called a community of believers to follow him. On Pentecost the
Holy Spirit descended on Jesus' apostles and disciples, and the
Church was formed. Members of this Christian community went
out into the world to testify in his name and offer his message of
hope. God's actions in Scripture indicate that we are created for
community, which we need to fulfill our destiny.

Our relationships with others define our roles within a particular community or group. A community is always associated with
relational identity. Interactions with others help us see our identity.
They give us a hint of who we are. We come to a deeper realization
of our identity because of our encounters with others.

Family life is at the center of relational identity. When my sisters,
brother, and I page through our family picture album, we remember the happy days of our childhood and youth. We observe each
member growing up and moving in a different life direction. The
pictures help us appreciate our close bonds, and the faith that is the
foundation of our lives. These pictures tell us that our family iden-

tity affected our individual stories, and the pictures help us appreciate how our family's identity influences who we are today.

Personal Identity and Hope

I learned as a young boy that I was made in God's image. Although I did not appreciate it at the time, it was my deepest identity and affected my subsequent actions. As a youth, I do not remember questioning my identity. I knew what it meant to be Catholic. Even when society and the Church changed in the 1960s, the core belief that I was made in God's likeness remained firm. My parents, family, parish, and Catholic schools shaped my personal identity.

My hope-filled childhood attitude grounded my faith and supported me during the difficulties that followed in life. The first defining moment in my life, my illness at age thirty-three described in Chapter One, jolted my sense of identity and threw me into a desert experience that lasted several years. God seemed a long way off, and I found it hard to experience God in the desert of my life. During this time, I identified with the Jewish people and their need for deliverance during their long years in the desert. Like them, the hope for my eventual liberation from sickness and exile kept me going.

As the months passed, I became closer to Jesus as I meditated on his time in the desert. During my illness I found strength in my story, my family story, the story of loving friends who visited me, and in the Christian story. God's love, reflected through these stories, gave me hope. Without this hope, I would have had little reason to endure the pain as days passed into months and years.

The story of my illness is rooted in a larger story (family, friends, Christian story), and this larger story is rooted in love. Basic beliefs and Christian hope influenced my story, as they influenced the larger story that engulfed me during this time. My beliefs enabled me to see my suffering within the wider context of Jesus' dying and rising. Hope in God's providence told me that eventually resurrection would come for me, even though I saw no such resurrection at the time. While I was sick I experienced God's love revealed in Jesus. I thought of concrete examples of such love in Jesus' teaching and actions. When he reached out to hurting people, I felt him also reaching out to me.

Jesus was very present to many different kinds of people in many different circumstances. I experienced a similar presence from people who were "other Christs" for me during my sickness. Their presence affected my personal identity and changed my view of God and myself. They gave me hope.

Context Identity and Hope

The context of our life shapes our personal and relational identity. For example, many Americans have a different attitude toward themselves than Asians or Africans have toward themselves. Our environment influences our view of ourselves and of others. Identification with elements of a particular environment is called contextual identity. Within the parameters of contextual identity, personal and relational identity develops.

We begin to develop our personality, internalize attitudes, and learn basic beliefs in our families. The home environment has the greatest influence on identity. The furniture, statues, pictures, and other furnishings in our homes can remind us of our Catholic faith and its beliefs. Until the first grade, my family and home environment were the only significant contexts that influenced me. My personal identity took root at home. My context expanded when I went to school, attended church, and played sports. Each situation affected my identity. My context expanded again when I went to the seminary, made new friends, and was ordained. Underpinning my growth and activities was the firm belief that God alone could bring me temporal happiness on earth and eternal happiness in heaven.

Hope, trust, love, and forgiveness help us better appreciate our core identity. While not as basic, our work and secular activities are also significant in our identity formation. Personal and relational identity always develops in real life contexts that involve a variety of experiences and activities. Christian core values, inherent in our story, offer us wisdom when we are challenged by materialistic values.

Hope in God

The Old Testament links hope with God's covenant promise of fidelity to the Jewish people. God's faithfulness gives rise to their messianic hope. The Jews understand the meaning of the messianic promise differently than Christians do.

When God called Abram from his homeland and promised to make his descendants as numerous as the sands of the seashore, something new happened. God entered history as a key player in humankind's future. From Abram forward, history became an important category of salvation.

In the Old Testament, hope is intimately joined with the story of the Jewish people. Yahweh's promise gives them the security and confidence they need to maintain their hope (Judg 18:9–10, Isa 32:9–10). Hope means that the people's future is entirely in Yahweh's hands. They believe that God will deliver them from oppression if they are faithful to God's commandments. One name for God is the "Hope of Israel" (Jer 14:8). Jews trust God's faithfulness, take refuge in God, expect a good future, and await God's coming with patience.

Christians believe that through Jesus' life, death, and resurrection, the messianic hope is fulfilled. By dying on the cross, Jesus established a new covenant between God and humankind. This covenant continues today and provides us with hope. Since Jesus lives in and through his Church, Christian hope and the Christian story are complimentary. Hope, based in Jesus' new covenant, is at the heart of God's ongoing walk with us.

New Testament passages describe God as the author, source, and object of hope. Many New Testament passages link hope with reaching one's final goal, often associated with Jesus' second coming (Heb 11:1—12:2) Christians cannot find true hope apart from Jesus.

Hope is intimately associated with God's story, the Jewish story, the Church's story and our stories. Jesus brought hope to all humankind through his death and resurrection. By internalizing his story, the Church's story, and our story, we can better appreciate this hope. Faith invites us to remember that God alone is our source of ultimate hope, something to remember in both good and difficult times.

We Christians are prophets of hope. We play a vital role in a society that needs hope. No better words express this hope than the first words of Mark's gospel, "The beginning of the Good News of Jesus Christ, the Son of God"(Mk 1:1). In these opening words, story and basic belief become one.

Points for Reflection

- What people and events from your childhood influenced your faith formation? What early memories do you have of learning about God?

- What do you remember about believing in God as a child? Did you see life, yourself, and this world as good and blessed by God? Why or why not?

- How did your parents influence your faith? Did they teach you to hope? If so, how?

- If someone asked you, "Who are you?" how would you answer? Would you mention a spiritual element to your identity? Why or why not?

- To whom do you belong? How does your belonging form your identity?

- Have you ever felt without hope? What helped you regain your hope and continue? How was faith involved?

- How important is your baptism to you? Explain.

- How has the context of your life (culture, nationality, economic status, etc.) shaped your personal and relational identity?

- What role does Christian hope play in your story? your family's story?

- If you believe that you are called to be a prophet of hope, what practical consequences does this have in your family? your professional work? your neighborhood? your parish?

- Which stories from your life do the stories in this chapter bring to mind?

- What is the most important insight that you gleaned from this chapter? Why does it have special significance? What does it tell you about your life?

Biblical Passages for Reflection

- What is "the good news of Jesus Christ, the Son of God" (Mk 1:1)?

- After Jesus' baptism, a voice from heaven said, "'You are my Son, the Beloved; with you I am well pleased'" (Mk 1:11). God says to you, "You are my beloved daughter, you are my beloved son; with you I am well pleased." What does this mean to you?

- "For our allotted time is the passing of a shadow, and there is no return from our death, because it is sealed up and no one turns back" (Wis 2:5). What do these words say to you? Where do you find your hope?

Action Steps

Genealogy. Inquire whether someone in the family has compiled a genealogy. If no one has, consider doing one. Gather family pictures of ancestral homes and religious celebrations and send them to other family members for Christmas.

Visit a sick or elderly person. Be a symbol of Christian hope by visiting someone in a nursing or healthcare facility. If you do not know anyone, ask a pastoral leader in your parish who ministers to the elderly to suggest a name or names. Visit the same person on a regular basis.

Writing project. Write a brief journal of key religious events that shaped your early faith formation and share it with your family members. What events or people brought you hope? Help your immediate family grow in appreciation of your religious heritage and the family's core values.

Faith testimony. At a large family gathering, invite elderly family members to share what their faith was like as children and young adults. Medals, holy cards, prayer books, and Bibles may trigger memories. Invite children or adolescents to take the lead in asking questions.

Conclusion

This book has considered story and basic belief. A book by William J. Bausch, *Storytelling: Imagination, and Faith* (New London, CT: Twenty-Third Publications, 1984), although written from a different perspective, reinforces many aspects of my book. His conclusions are the headings for my last reflections on story and basic beliefs.

Stories Introduce Us to Sacramental Presences

As stories touch the core of life, they introduce us to a deeper awareness of God's sacramental presence in creation, the animal world, and human relationships. Beautiful and painful experiences from birth to death disclose a "something more" that we cannot fully capture in words. Without the story we cannot recall the transcendent God whose presence is manifested in a child's birth, a wedding celebration, or a parent's death. The biblical revelation of the Old and New Testaments reveal God's special presence, anticipated by God's presence throughout nature.

Stories Are Always More Important than Facts

The cold facts of science, computer technology, or mathematics cannot capture the depths of a powerful story. In the presence of mystery, disclosed in a story, scientific facts manifest their limitations. While both story and facts are necessary for survival, the profound wisdom of a story underpins whatever science offers us to make our life better.

Applied to faith, this means that the truths contained in the Bible are more profound than their explanations. The gospel accounts of Jesus' crucifixion, death, and resurrection goes beyond any factual explanation. These stories convey profound truths. The facts they represent, while setting the foundation of the story, are largely unknown.

Stories Remain Normative

In a world where money, status, and power rule the day, stories touch life's core. Personal and family stories are the foundation for our personal, relational, and contextual identity. Through them we come to recognize that relationships with our parents, children, spouses, and siblings are more important than the house we live in, our position in life, or income. Since stories reflect the core of who we are, they have deep significance. Their wisdom contains the ultimate norms in our search for identity and life's meaning.

In a Christian context, our spirituality, catechesis, liturgy, and theology reflect the insights and celebrate the core beliefs of the story of God's dealings with the Jewish people and of God's sending Jesus to redeem us from our sins. The Old Testament story grounded the laws that Jesus followed as a devout Jew. His story is normative for succeeding Christian generations. The Hebrew-Christian story set the foundation for the Church and the development of Christian tradition.

Traditions Evolve through Stories

Catholic Tradition (with a capital "T") is the living faith and practice of the Catholic community from early Christian times until today. From the beginning Christians developed their beliefs and practices in light of the core elements of Jesus' story. What was in line with his teaching they accepted; what was not they rejected.

It took time for the Church to clarify the essentials of the Christian tradition. For example, various opinions about three persons in God arose in the early centuries. The Council of Constantinople in 381 AD settled these controversies when it affirmed definitively the equality of three persons in God, solidifying the Church's belief in the Trinity. From Christianity's beginning, Jesus' story and its Trinitarian understanding were normative.

Stories Precede and Produce the Church

The Church was formed by the early apostles and disciples who heard, accepted, and followed Jesus' teaching. The story of his life, death, and resurrection was the norm. After Pentecost they recognized his continued presence among them. They realized their calling as Church to center their lives on him and his story in order to authentically share his gospel with all peoples.

The energy and beliefs inherent in Jesus' story rooted the disciples' faith and its spread throughout the world. The oral telling of this story led to the written New Testament. Evidence of the power of Jesus' story is found in Paul's writings and the other letters, the gospels, Acts, and Revelation. The Church received its dynamism from Jesus' story. This story continues to breathe life into developing local churches throughout the world and to energize parishes, religious communities, lay associations, Christian schools, families, and individuals everywhere.

Stories Imply Censure

Sometimes correction or censure is necessary for an individual, a family, or a parish. The Catholic story reflects the Church's core beliefs and practices. Whenever teaching or practice deviate from it, the community committed to preserving the story intact says "no" to them. Those responsible for keeping the story in its authentic form must respond at times with censure, if someone claiming to represent the story actually deviates from it. When individuals or communities interpret the core message of Jesus differently than the authentic Tradition of the Church, communities faithful to his original story must reject such teachings.

In the Catholic Church, the chief authority responsible for preserving Jesus' story and the Church's story from error is the pope and the bishops acting in union with him (the magisterium). Holy Spirit's presence in the Church to the end of time guards it from error and assures Church members that the authentic story of Jesus continues intact.

Stories Produce Theology

Theology is a community's or individual's formulation of God's dealing with humankind as disclosed through holy people, sacred writings, and traditions. It involves a well-developed consideration of how God manifests laws and divine designs for humans in the revealed truths and traditions of religious people. Early people conveyed instruction from God or the gods through stories that their ancestors received from the creator in the beginning. Often these took the form of creation stories that contained a community's most basic beliefs. For example, Hindu and Buddhist sacred writings reflect the truths that their members, leaders, and scholars use for prayer and scholarship. From an analysis of these stories' core beliefs and the community's interpretation of them, theology emerges.

Jewish and Christian theologians study the revealed truths of the Old and New Testaments and draw systematic conclusions from them in light of their traditions. In this process, theological differences emerge because of the different ways individuals or particular communities interpret holy writings and traditions.

In each instance, theology springs from the fundamental stories of each community as the community's tradition interprets them. To be authentic, every theological approach must return to its community's basic story and traditions for its truth, energy, and core meaning. In Catholic theology, the story of God's dealings with humankind, revealed through the Old and New Testaments, is interpreted within the living Tradition of the Church. Both the Scriptures and Tradition constitute the two necessary fonts of God's revelation.

Stories Produce Many Theologies

Different communities often see their core stories and traditions through particular lenses. The various Christian communities that compiled the four gospels interpreted the core story of Jesus from different perspectives. In each instance, however, they remained faithful to the basic or deepest aspect of Jesus' story, revealed in his life, teaching, death, and resurrection. The theologies that flow from each of the four gospels manifest the different fundamental orientations of the communities that formulated these gospels and the audiences for whom they were intended.

Through history Christian communities interpreted Jesus' core message differently and produced different theologies. Catholic and Protestant theologians have reached different conclusions when considering theological issues such as grace, nature of the Church, and authority.

The Western (Roman) and Eastern Catholic Churches, in communion with Rome, remain true to Jesus' core message, but differ in the focus of their basic beliefs, rituals, and traditions.

Stories Produce Ritual and Sacrament

The ritual patterns that flow from stories are their natural outgrowth. Families remember and celebrate core family experiences, like birth, marriage, and death. They are ritualized through family gatherings and other events. Ritual patterns also celebrate core experiences, reflected in the stories of a nation or of a religious community of men or women. People celebrate the anniversaries of national heroes and Church heroes. Rituals are natural outgrowths of stories. Stories precede ritual actions; ritual actions flow from stories.

Sacraments are sacred manifestations of the divine. They ritually enact and celebrate key aspects of the Christian story. Without the story, sacraments lose their power to focus a community of believers around core beliefs and practices.

Stories Are History

Without stories, no real history would exist. History is the story of people, not the mere repetition of facts. Every person is a living story with a history. The Judeo-Christian story makes possible salvation history. Yahweh called Abram and formed a people around him. The history of the Jews recounts a series of events. These events are remembered through stories told for thousands of years. These stories give them their identity and call them to what they are to become. Christian history centers on Jesus. The Church formed around belief in him and his mission as the Son of God. This history contains the stories of saints and sinners alike. It offers people of every age the core Christian beliefs and practices that recall the past and build a path into the future.

Conclusion

Stories point us toward life's meaning. Stories move us to recognize the importance of practicing Christian virtues, living reflectively, and internalizing our basic beliefs. Stories generate new stories. The emerging process of living, reflecting, discovering, and living more fully, mirrors the gospels. Personalization of this process engenders deep Christian virtues as living theology (Jesus incarnate). The Christian community and Tradition keeps our story, especially its defining moments, in balance.

The road of story and basic belief is a solid path to follow in our role as prophets of hope, rooted in faith and inflamed with love.